THE EARLY SEVENTEENTH-CENTURY YORK BOOK TRADE AND JOHN FOSTER'S INVENTORY OF 1616

JOHN BARNARD and MAUREEN BELL

LEEDS
THE LEEDS PHILOSOPHICAL AND LITERARY SOCIETY LTD
FEBRUARY 1994

Proceedings of the Leeds Philosophical and Literary Society, Literary and Historical Section, Vol. XXIV, Part II, pp. 17–132

The Leeds Philosophical and Literary Society Ltd.,
City Museum,
Calverley Street,
Leeds LS1 3AA

Editor, Literary and Historical Section

IAN MOXON, M.A.

University of Leeds

British Library Cataloguing-in-Publication Data:
a catalogue record for this book is available from the British Library.

ISBN 1–870737–06–7

Printed in Great Britain by W. S. Maney and Son Ltd.   Leeds

CONTENTS

		PAGE
List of Figures	. . . .	v
List of Tables	. . . .	v
Acknowledgements	. . . .	vii
Introduction	. . . .	1
The Book Trade in the Minster Yard	. . . .	1
A Family Business	. . . .	7
Buyers of Books in York and Foster's Debtors	. . . . .	16
The Book-Stock Inventory	. . . .	22
1. Subject Categories	. . . .	25
2. Prices	. . . .	31
3. Age and Origin of Stock	. . . . . .	34
i. *STC* Books	. . . .	34
ii. Continental Books	. . . .	35
A Basis for Comparison?	. . . .	37
Conclusion	. . . .	41
Appendix 1:	Corrections and Additions to Robert Davies's Transcript of John Foster's Inventory (York, 1616)	43
Appendix 2:	Identification of Works in the Inventory of John Foster's Books	53
Appendix 3:	John Foster's Appraisers and Debtors	97
Appendix 4:	The Will of Anthony Foster (BHI, Exchequer Probate Records, York City Deanery, July 1610)	105
Appendix 5:	The Will of Margaret Foster (BHI, Probate Registers, vol. 32, fos. 392^b–93^a, March 1613)	107

FIGURES

PAGE

1a. 'The South Crosse of the Cathedrall Church of St Peter of Yorke', plate
62 [bis = 63] of Daniel King, *The Cathedrall and Conventvall Churches of
England and Wales orthographically delineated* (London, 1656)   .   .   .   5

1b. The stationer's shop, detail of Figure 1a   6

2. Map showing domicile of John Foster's debtors (1616)   18

TABLES

PAGE

1. The families of Anthony Foster and John Foster   8

2. The families of Richard Foster and Mark Foster   14

3. John Foster's debtors: analytical table   17

4. Relative values of the several kinds of book inventoried   .   .   .   23

5. Format of books: quantity and value   24

6. Foster's entire stock by subject category   25

7. Foster's entire stock in three main groupings   26

8. Average price of books per copy for each subject category   .   .   .   27

9. Comparison of Foster's prices with prices available from two other
    published lists   32

10. *STC* books by date: quantity and value   35

11. Continental books by date: quantity and value   36

12. Foster's inventory compared with other York inventories   .   .   .   38

13. Foster's inventory compared with inventories from other provincial
     towns   39

14. Comparison of Foster's stock with those of other provincial booksellers   41

ACKNOWLEDGEMENTS

We are indebted to the Leverhulme Trust without whose support this work could not have been undertaken. We are also grateful to the School of English, University of Leeds, for the study leave which allowed John Barnard time for research.

We have received generous help and advice from individuals and institutions throughout our exploration of John Foster's business. We would like to thank Bernard Barr of York Minster Library in particular for his invaluable encouragement and expert guidance to the kinds of archival evidence available. We would also like to thank M. Dorrington and the other staff of York Minster Library, Mrs. R. J. Freedman of York City Archives, Christopher Sheppard and Dr. Oliver Pickering of the Brotherton Collection, University of Leeds, and P. S. Morrish and Malcolm Davis, Special Collections, University of Leeds. David Pearson of the Victoria and Albert Museum gave timely advice and additional leads. The staff of the following institutions were uniformly helpful: Borthwick Historical Institute (University of York), Local Studies Collection (Nottinghamshire County Library), Lincolnshire Archives, Norfolk Records Office, Public Records Office (Chancery Lane), and the University of Nottingham library. Dr. Terry Screeton of the Computing Service gave important help in the early stages of the project, and Anne Tindall once again turned difficult copy into clearly presented text. Paul Morgan's work on the provincial trade has been a constant help, as has his advice, and we are grateful for the generosity of Ian Maxted.

Ian Moxon's meticulous and patient work as editor, which continued right up to the very last moment, has been extremely helpful. He has saved us from inconsistencies and errors and has much improved the presentation of our text and tables.

Finally, we would like to acknowledge the support given by Hermione Lee and George and Jessica Parfitt.

JOHN BARNARD
MAUREEN BELL

Introduction

Transcripts of the inventories of John Foster's goods and book stock made in 1616 were published by Robert Davies in 1868.[1] His transcription is careful but it silently omits some classes of entries in the book stock, and he chose not to publish the list of forty-three debtors given at the end of the inventory. The omissions are mainly of bibles, service books, and psalms, which are repetitive for the reader, but were of substantial commercial importance to the bookseller. The whole inventory is remarkable for its detail, giving individual titles, format, and prices, as well as his debtors. A fresh analysis of the book-stock inventory, coupled with an analysis of Foster's debtors and further archival evidence, gives a more detailed account of Foster's own business and of the York book trade in the early years of the seventeenth century than previously possible. Briefly, Anthony Foster was in business from *c.* 1580 to his death in 1610; his business was taken over by his cousin, John Foster, from 1610 until his own death in 1616, aged thirty-two.[2] This synopsis suggests that John Foster's inventory tells as much about his predecessor's business as about his own brief career.

The Book Trade in the Minster Yard

As a regional centre, York had a large population of around 10,000 in 1600, rising to 12,000 in 1630, and the city played a leading role in secular and ecclesiastical administration.[3] Recent estimates of population size suggest a population for the first decade of the seventeenth century of around 11,000 and overall a continuing increase despite the severity of the plague in 1604.[4] A prosperous market town, York was the social and trading centre of a large rural area and attracted an increasing number of gentry as residents: by 1642 there were 697 gentry families in York, a larger concentration than anywhere else excepting Devon.[5] The large numbers of higher clergy, lawyers, civil servants, and other professionals who serviced the institutions of ecclesiastical, royal, and civic power congregated in the liberties of the city: around the Minster, the castle, and the King's Manor. Doctors and schoolmasters also tended to live and work in the same areas and most, if not all, of the stationers and booksellers who catered for this professional élite had their shops in the liberties too.

---

[1] R. Davies, *A Memoir of the York Press with Notices of Authors, Printers, and Stationers in the Sixteenth, Seventeenth, and Eighteenth Centuries* (London, 1868; rptd. York, 1988, with introduction by Bernard Barr).

[2] R. B. McKerrow *et al.*, *A Dictionary of Printers and Booksellers in England, Scotland and Ireland ... 1557–1640* (London, 1910); reprinted in H. R. Plomer *et al.*, *Dictionaries of the Printers and Booksellers who were at work in England, Scotland and Ireland 1557–1775* (London, 1977).

[3] P. M. Tillott, *A History of Yorkshire: the city of York*, Victoria History of the Counties of England (London, 1961), p. 162.

[4] D. M. Palliser, *Tudor York* (Oxford, 1979), pp. 112–13, 125.

[5] Tillott, op. cit. (note 3), p. 165; J. T. Cliffe, 'The Yorkshire gentry on the eve of civil war', Ph.D. thesis (University of London, 1960), pp. 5, 10, 88.

Trading within the liberties meant that the tradesmen were not under the obligation and expense of becoming freemen of the city, and in the course of the sixteenth century fewer and fewer members of the book trade became freemen. Of the forty-three stationers who can now be identified as active before 1616, twenty-three became freemen, ten by patrimony, but none of them after 1589.[6] By 1603 not a single stationer was a freeman. Davies notes the city council's attempt to re-establish the trade within the city. On 20 July 1603 the council

... agreed that Thomas Gubbyn stacyoner shalbe maide a freman of this Cittie for twenty mkes accordynge to the order yet not wthstanding in regard ther is none other of the same trade that are also maide fremen of this Cittie, and that he is thought to be skilfull & Cunninge in the saide occupacon It is agreed that xx^{tie} nobles of the saide xx^{tie} marks shalbe rebated and given him backe againe, and that he shall paie xx^{tie} nobles, viz xiii^s iiij^d in hand, and xx^s yearlie at Pentecost and mtgmass by even porcons the first payement to begin at Pentecost nexte puttinge in suertycs for the same[7]

Gubbin, a London bookseller, whose first known imprint is dated 1587, certainly set up business in York but was back in London in 1614 with a shop near Holborn conduit.[8] In 1608 the council made a similar arrangement with Richard Foster on 30 January, and asked that he pay 33s. 4d. 'at the tyme of his enfranchestment', renewing the arrangement on 10 December 1610.[9] A little later, on 31 August 1614, Gilbert Stork, stationer, asked the council to 'licence' him 'to vse and exercise the same occupation for two or thre yere untill it shall please God to inable him to make hymself free of this Corporacon'. The council on this occasion allowed him the 'libertye to vse the same traide for one yere next Comencing within this Cittie' but, unusually, made no mention of any payment.[10] Stork stayed in York for at least two

[6] E. G. Duff identifies twenty-seven in *A Century of the English Book Trade . . .* (London, 1905), and a further five are listed in McKerrow, op. cit. (note 2). Davies adds Thomas Gubbin and Gilbert Stork (op. cit. (note 1), pp. 33, 342). Anthony Foster's will (see Appendix 4) adds Roger Jackman, stationer, while the Chamberlain's Rolls of York Minster identify William Blanchard as a stationer (see Appendix 3). McKerrow did not consult F. Collins (ed.), *Register of the Freemen of the City of York from the City Records vol. II 1559–1759*, The Publications of the Surtees Society, 102 for 1899 (Durham, 1900). This adds six further names: 1562 'Thomas Robinson, stacyoner, fil. Jacobi Robynson, merchant' (p. 5); 1574 'Stephanus Bekwith, stacyner' (p. 15); 1577 'Thomas Smirthwaite, stacioner' (p. 19); 1584 'Willelmus Jackson, stacioner' (p. 29); 1589 'Thomas Richardson, stacioner, fil. Thomas Richardson, stacioner' (p. 32); 1589 'Robertus Nixson, stacioner, fil. Petri Nixson, bladsmyth' (p. 32). A systematic search for any extant wills of these members of the York book trade might give further information about its development in the city.
[7] York City Archives (hereafter abbreviated to YCA), House Books, vol. 32, fo. 281^a. The House Books occasionally give similar permission to men of other trades, stipulating the payment required, in addition to the stationers noted above.
[8] *A Short-Title Catalogue of Books Printed in England, Scotland, & Ireland and of English Books Printed Abroad 1475–1640*, compiled by A. W. Pollard & G. R. Redgrave, 2nd edn. rev. by W. A. Jackson, F. S. Ferguson and K. F. Pantzer, 3 vols. (London, 1976–91) (hereafter abbreviated to *STC*), vol. III. Gubbin was still in York in 1609: he christened two children there, the second on 19 September 1609 (F. Collins (ed.), *The Registers of St. Michael le Belfrey, York, Part I 1565–1653*, Publications of the Yorkshire Parish Register Society, 1 (York, 1899)).
[9] YCA, House Books, vol. 33, fos. 151^a, 227^a. The reference to his 'enfranchestment' is puzzling: it cannot refer to completion of his apprenticeship. For his possible relationship with the Fosters trading in the Minster Yard, see pp. 13 and 15.
[10] YCA, House Books, vol. 34, fo. 40^a.

years: he had a son in March 1615, and was one of John Foster's appraisers in 1616.[11] The motives of the city council are not clear. Davies is probably right to say that they wanted to encourage the establishment of the book trade within that part of the city under their jurisdiction.[12] If so, they were unsuccessful. None of the three stationers established himself well enough to become a freeman.

The Minster Yard, on the other hand, had an increasing population of members of the book trade from 1572/73, the first year in which the bookshop which eventually became John Foster's was rented. Two sets of the Minster's rental accounts which use the 'Minster Yard' or 'Garth' as a subdivision give a clear picture of the book trade's concentration in the Minster Yard.[13] The chamberlain's accounts for 1572/73 contain the first record of a 'newe builded' shop dwelt in by the 'Staconer'. It is always mentioned in an entry which includes three other shops also rented by the stationer:

Item for the halfe yeres rente of the newe builded Shoppe wherein the Staconer dwelleth due at Mydsomer next comynge xxvj⁵ viijᵈ. Item for halfe yeres rente of the three[?] builded Shoppes within the Minster yarde Due at Mydsomer next comynge xxxj⁵ viij[?]ᵈ[14]

This formula, including the rental figures with minor variations, is repeated in all the extant readable accounts until 1607/08, when 'Anthonie Foster' is for the first time named as the stationer.[15] In contrast the Fabric Roll which survives for 1571/72 records the rental of no fewer than ten properties in the Minster Yard. Unfortunately no trades or occupations are given, but the names of two men known to have belonged to the book trade occur. Thomas Richardson paid a yearly rent of 10s. 'for a Shoppe' as did John Gowthwaite.[16] Three other shops were rented at 10s., one at 8s. 8d., one at 2s. and another at 1s. Two tenements were rented at £1 and £1 6s. 8d.

Forty years later the balance of rentals recorded by Chamberlain's Rolls and the Fabric Rolls had changed substantially. Only two Fabric Rolls are preserved for the first two decades of the seventeenth century, those for 1607/08 and 1611/12: they record only eight and six rentals in the Minster Yard respectively.[17] Both are only partially readable, but enough of that for 1607/08 can be seen to show that the rentals

[11] See Appendix 3.
[12] Davies, op. cit. (note 1), p. 33.
[13] The liberty of the Minster extended to properties owned by the canons in neighbouring streets like Stonegate and Petergate. However, the rent rolls of the vicars choral, which are arranged by street, do not mention the Minster Yard, and contain no names recognizable as those of stationers in the obvious streets for the period 1616/17 (York Minster Library — hereafter abbreviated to YML — Vc. 6/2/113–14).
[14] YML, Chamberlain's Rolls, E.1/91. That the stationer usually rented both the stationer's shop and the 'three [?] builded Shoppes' is shown by a single entry in 1633/34, when the stationer's shop was rented separately from the others (see note 44 below).
[15] YML, Chamberlain's Rolls, E.1/110.
[16] YML, Fabric Rolls, E.3/52, which needs to be read against E.3/51 (1569/70). In 1579/80 Gowthwaite is described as the 'late' tenant. D. M. Palliser and D. G. Selwyn show that Thomas Richardson, made free in 1533/34, died in 1575 ('The stock of a York stationer, 1538', *The Library*, 5th series, 27 (1972), 207–19). Names can be perpetuated in the Fabric Rolls long after an individual's death: in this case Richardson was succeeded by his son, also Thomas, who in turn freed his own son Thomas by patrimony in 1589. It was presumably the last who apprenticed his son to a London stationer in 1600 (McKerrow, op. cit. (note 2)). There were, therefore, probably three Thomas Richardsons active in the book trade between 1533 and 1616.
[17] YML, Fabric Rolls, E.3/62/1–2.

charged are identical to those of 1572/73, and that none of the names resembles that of any known stationer or bookseller, certainly not that of Thomas Richardson.

Where the Fabric Rolls show a slight decline, the chamberlain's accounts show a sharp increase in the number of rentals in the yard. In 1572/73 the stationer's shop and the 'three[?] builded Shoppes' were the only ones; by 1610, the year Anthony Foster died, the accounts show a further eight rentals, which had risen to eleven by 1616, when his successor died.[18] The chamberlain's stock of houses, tenements, and shops was rented by a mixture of classes and trades. A house earlier leased by Henry Swinburn (1560?–1623), the ecclesiastical lawyer, was occupied by William Holmes, gentleman, for a yearly rent of £2; at the other extreme, William Lamplough rented a shop for 8d. a year. The highest rent of £3 6s. 8d. was paid by Matthew Holloway, gentleman, for two tenements. John Allanson, a saddler, rented a tenement (£2 p.a.) as did the scrivener, William Hickes (£1 16s. 4d.). If Anthony Foster and his successor were paying rent for the leases of both the stationer's shop (£2 13s. 4d. a year) and the 'three[?] builded Shoppes' (£3 3s. 4d. a year), rather than sub-letting the latter, they were the chamberlain's most important tenants. The rent of the stationer's shop alone is proof of the substantial scale of their business, as is clear from a comparison with the rents paid by other stationers and bookbinders. In 1571/72 John Gowthwaite and Thomas Richardson were each paying 10s. a year into the fabric accounts. In 1611 Thomas Gubbin began paying the chamberlain a yearly rent of only 4s. for 'two other new builded shopps wth the Chambers over them at the west end of the minster lane'.[19]

The evidence gives an indication of the minimum number of people involved in the York book trade in 1616. Apart from John Foster himself, there were two of his appraisers, William Blanchard and Gilbert Stork. Roger Jackman, who administered Margaret Foster's will in 1613 and is mentioned in both her will and that of her husband, was also probably still in business. If the Richard Foster whose shop was 'near the Minster gate' in 1626 is the same as the Richard Foster who petitioned the city in 1608 and 1609 to set up in business, a further name is added.[20] Thomas Richardson, the third York stationer of that name, apprenticed his son to a London stationer in 1600 and may still have been active in 1616.[21] Up to six stationers, then, had their businesses in the Minster Yard in the year of John Foster's death.

Where their shops were located is certain only in the case of Foster himself. William Blanchard may have taken over the two shops in the 'minster lane' rented by Thomas Gubbin in 1611. These are described as 'late' in Gubbin's tenure in 1612, but as the rent continued to be paid until 1617 the shops seem to have been in use. In 1618/19 William Blanchard, stationer, appears for the first time as renting a 'house and two

---

[18] YML, Fabric Rolls, E.1/112–23.
[19] YML, Chamberlain's Rolls, E.1/122, uses this description, which varies slightly from earlier descriptions (YML, Chamberlain's Rolls, E.1/114ff.).
[20] STC 6441, Edmund Deane's *Spadacrene Anglica. Or, the English spaw-fountaine. Being a briefe treatise of the acide, or tart fountaine in the forest of Knaresborow* (London, 1626).
[21] McKerrow, op. cit. (note 2). On the Richardsons, see note 16 above.

The South Crosse of the Cathedrall Church of St Peter of Yorke.

Ne vestigium quoq intereat. hoc ꝫ posuit. Iohannes Brooke

Figure 1a. 'The South Crosse of the Cathedrall Church of St Peter of Yorke', plate 62 [bis = 63] of Daniel King, *The Cathedrall and Conventvall Churches of England and Wales orthographically delineated* (London, 1656).

Figure 1b.   The stationer's shop, detail of Figure 1a.

shops with th appurtenances in the Minster garth' for 3*s*. 6*d*. a year.[22] The additional house and lower rate means either that Blanchard was renting another property while Gubbin's shops stood empty, or that as a local man he was able to negotiate better terms. The two shops elsewhere in the Minster Yard which had been rented by Thomas Richardson and John Gowthwaite in 1571/72 may have remained within the trade, and Bookbinders' Alley by the Minster gates had given the trade premises since the medieval period.[23]

The 'newe builded' stationer's shop was 'on the West side of the minster doore' and the 'three[?] builded Shoppes' were on the 'East syde'.[24] These buildings are depicted in some detail in Daniel King's engraving of the 'South Crosse', first published in 1656 in *The Cathedrall and Conventvall Churches of England and Wales orthographically delineated* (see Figures 1a and b).[25] Hollar's engraving of the south front for the third

[22] YML, Chamberlain's Rolls, E.1/115–26. Blanchard's rental is recorded from 1618 to 1620 (YML, Chamberlain's Rolls, E.1/125–27); his name does not appear in the next extant roll for 1621 (YML, Chamberlain's Rolls, E.1/128); it reappears in the surviving rolls for 1625/26, 1628, and 1633/34 (YML, Chamberlain's Rolls, E.1/132–36). He may have been related to the John Blanchard who rented a house in the yard in 1588/89 (YML, Chamberlain's Rolls, E.1/100). Confusingly, in the years 1608–18 John Blanchard's name alternates with that of John Jackson, leatherdresser. Since both paid the same rent, 3*s*., and never appear together, it is assumed to be the same house (YML, Chamberlain's Rolls, E.1/112–24). Further on William Blanchard, see Appendix 3.

[23] A. Raine, *Mediaeval York: a topographical survey based on original sources* (London, 1955), p. 34.

[24] YML, Chamberlain's Rolls, E.1/100 (1588/89).

[25] King's engraving was included in the second edition of Dugdale's *Monasticon Anglicanum* (London, 1718), plate 85, where it can be conveniently compared with Hollar's engraving of 1673.

volume of Sir William Dugdale's *Monasticon* published in 1673 is more accurate than King's, but clears away the accretions, achieving in art what the king had ordered in 1633 but which was not effected until they were pulled down by Thomas Gale, dean from 1697 to 1702.[26] As a result Daniel King's rather approximate engraving is the only one to include the shops. The stationer's shop is on the left, that is, the west side of the south entrance to the Minster, and is earlier than any English example given in Taubert's *Bibliopola*.[27] The building is clearly both a house and a shop. It is a structure of three bays with pitched roofs backing against the Minster walls, two storeys high (the two little windows at the top of the left- and right-hand bays cannot have been for a third level of garret rooms since the height would not allow it). Lattice windows are shown, and the bookshop itself is on the right, nearest the Minster door. The stall-board, with a large rectangular opening above, is to the right of the door, the only entrance shown. There appears to be a penthouse projecting forward over the stall-board and door, which runs the length of the frontage, with a room built out under it in the left-hand bay. The house had perhaps as many as six rooms including the shop. The shops on the right share the same improvised architecture, and three doors are clearly visible. These shops, like the stationer's, have tall narrow chimneys, and both sets of buildings go round either side of the two inner buttresses. Given Daniel King's freedom with his subject and the subsequent changes to the stairs and the level of the paving, it is impossible to give precise measurements. The stationer's shop, to judge from the engraving, was between twenty-four and thirty feet across, depending how far the building reached towards the outer buttress. If the engraving's proportions are reliable, this would make the height between twelve (impossibly low?) and fifteen feet.[28] Its depth can only be guessed at: perhaps twelve or fifteen feet also? Since the rent was unchanged between its first renting in 1572/73 and 1634, its structure can have changed little, though the frontage under the left part of the penthouse may be an extension. The stationer's shop, first built eighty years earlier, was probably structurally unchanged when King made his engraving of 1656.

A Family Business

Anthony Foster was in business in the stationer's house from at least 1580/81. In that year the Fabric Rolls record two payments for psalters 'wth geneua psalmes' from one 'Foster', named as Anthony in the following year when he supplied the Minster with 'xxxiij queres of royall paper at xij[d] the quere and for the binding the same into xviij bookes for prickinge of songs for the quere' for £2 4s. The payment of 5s. to 'Anthonie

[26] The order was the king's, but was probably inspired by Archbishop Laud, who accompanied Charles I on his visit. See K. M. Longley and J. Ingamells, *The Beautifullest Church: York Minster 1472–1972* . . . (York, 1972), p. 11. Drake remarks on the removal of the shops: '. . . the worthy dean Gale . . . suffered the leases to run out, pulled down the houses and cleaned this part of the church from the scurf which it had contracted by the smoke proceeding from these dwellings' (F. Drake, *Eboracum* . . . (London, 1736), p. 486).
[27] S. Taubert, *Bibliopola* . . ., 2 vols. (Hamburg and London, 1966).
[28] See the ground plan, with a scale, in J. Britton, *The History and Antiquities of the Metropolitical Church of York* . . . (London, 1819).

Table 1.   The families of Anthony Foster and John Foster

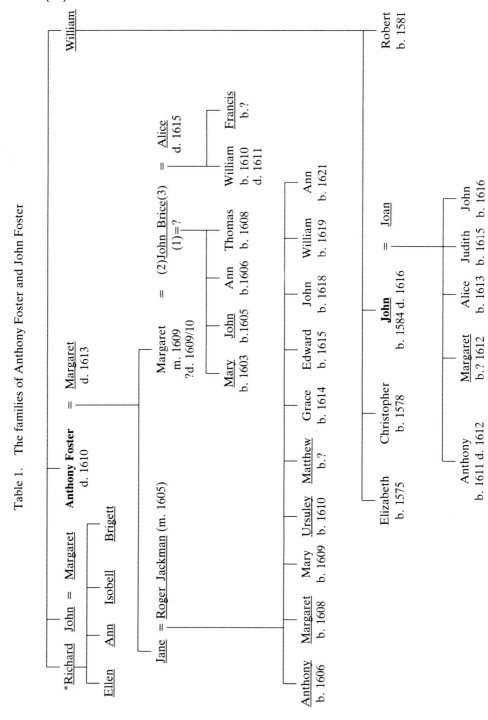

* Names underlined appear either in the will of Anthony, or of Margaret, or of both.

M^r marshe his man for a Com*mun*ion boke' in 1578/79 means that he may have set up on his own as early as 1579, or more likely that he took over from his master, the stationer named 'Marshe' who earlier sold the Minster three psalm books in 1568/69.[29] Mr. Marshe was, then, in all probability the first tenant of the stationer's shop by the south entrance to the Minster.

By the time of his death in 1610 Anthony Foster had been in business in the Minster Yard for some thirty years. That he had a close relationship with some of the local clergy is attested by the appearance of his name as witness to the will of Edward Swaine, vicar choral, in 1585. Swaine also delivered into Foster's hands the sum of £50 5s. 8d. to be paid out according to Swaine's instructions.[30] Foster was thus a sufficiently established figure in the community around the Minster to be entrusted with another's cash. The relatively high rental paid on the stationer's shop and the other three shops suggests that his business was consistently profitable. In the lay subsidies for 1596 and 1600 he was assessed at £3 8s.[31] The details of his will, made in 1610, give a clear picture of his assets and of his relationships both with family members and with other stationers in York.[32]

The will points to strong connections between the Fosters and a family called Marsh. (In the following discussion it may be helpful to refer to the tentative family tree of Anthony and John Foster presented in Table 1.) The two children of Thomas Marsh, Anthony and Margaret, had the first call on Anthony Foster's care when he made his will in 1610. He left each of Thomas Marsh's children £20, the largest legacies in the will apart from that to his business successor, John Foster. In addition he made provision for their education. Thomas's son Anthony was to be educated by John Brice (one of the will's supervisors) and his daughter Margaret was to be educated by Anthony Foster's wife.[33] The position of these provisions, coming first in the list of legacies, and the age of the children (Anthony Marsh was about thirteen years old, and Margaret fifteen) suggest that Marsh had willed the guardianship of the children to Foster.[34] The fact that the children have the same names as Anthony Foster and his wife, Margaret, may mean that the couple were godparents to the Marsh children.

---

[29] YML, Fabric Rolls, E.3/57–58, 50. There are two more payments to Foster than are reported by J. Raine (ed.), *The Fabric Rolls of York Minster with an Appendix of Illustrative Documents*, The Publications of the Surtees Society, 35 for 1858 (Durham, 1859). 'Foster' can be clearly if faintly read in E.3/57 (Raine, op. cit. (note 29), no. LVII) and there is another entry in E.3/61 (1587/88). Raine on occasions slightly rewords his selection from the minor expenses, and regularly uses old-style dating (which accounts for the differences between his dates and those given here).

[30] C. Cross (ed.), *York Clergy Wills 1520–1600: I Minster Clergy*, Borthwick Texts and Calendars: Records of the Northern Province, 10 (York, 1984), pp. 135–37. Swaine's will is dated 6 June 1585 (probated 2 March 1587/88).

[31] YCA, Subsidy Book 1558–1600, fos. 200^b, 222^b.

[32] For the wills of both Anthony and Margaret Foster, discussed below, see Appendices 4 and 5.

[33] Brice is described as 'cosen' in Margaret Foster's will. He is probably the 'Johannes Brice, innholder', freed by patrimony in 1604 (F. Collins (ed.), op. cit. (note 6), p. 51.

[34] *International Genealogical Index of the Church of Christ of Latter Day Saints* (Salt Lake City, 1981–) (hereafter abbreviated to *IGI*). Anthonye, son of Thomas Marshe, christened 14 May 1597; Margarett, daughter of Thomas Marshe, christened 16 January 1595, both in the parish of St. Michael le Belfrey.

Margaret Foster's will of 1613 makes further provision for the two children, adding another £40 to the £40 left to them by Anthony which had not yet been paid.[35]

The Thomas Marsh in Anthony Foster's will is the bookbinder and stationer recorded by McKerrow as being active between 1590 and 1597.[36] He is not the son of the Mr. Marsh for whom Anthony Foster worked until 1579 or 1580, but the son of William Marsh, husbandman, of Marfleet near Hull. On 25 September 1590 'Tho. Marshe stacioner or booke binder of York' signed a twenty-year lease with St. John's College, Cambridge, for a tenement and land previously occupied by his father. He renewed it on 18 October 1597 and was allowed to alienate the lease on 15 February 1599.[37] Since his father first rented a tenement and land from the college in 1560, the York stationer's family originated from rural Humberside and had William and Thomas as family names.[38] The probability is that the Fosters and Marshes were related, and that Anthony Foster took over the stationer's business from a relative. This would explain his otherwise puzzling legacy to 'Agnes Marsh late wife of Thomas Marsh', who was to receive 'fortie shillings'. Agnes is most likely the widow of the 'Mr. Marshe' whose business Anthony Foster took over in 1579/80, in which case he was also called Thomas.

Intermarriage involves the Fosters with another family in the York book trade. In his will Anthony twice mentioned Roger Jackman, whom he identified as a stationer. Jackman owed Anthony £11, which the latter directed should be paid to Jackman's children, £8 to Anthonie Jackman and £3 to the daughter, Margaret. The recurrence of these two names is suggestive of a family relationship, and parish records bear this out. Jackman was married to a Jane Foster in 1605, and the children were christened in St. Michael le Belfrey in 1606 (Anthonie) and 1608 (Margaret), making them about four and two years old respectively at the time of Anthony Foster's will.[39] No birth or christening record for Jane Foster has been found, but the coincidence of the Christian names of the Jackman children with the Christian names of Anthony and Margaret Foster, the generous legacies to the children, and additional legacies both to Jane herself and to a child she was carrying, should it be born alive, all point to the likelihood that Jane was Anthony Foster's daughter. In appointing Roger Jackman one of the supervisors of his will, Anthony was probably entrusting its administration to his son-in-law. In Margaret's will of 1613 the Jackmans are again prominent. Roger Jackman is described by Margaret as 'my Cosen' and the Jackman children are important beneficiaries: Margaret Jackman was to receive £7, two more Jackman children £4 each, and the will directs that after John Foster's death the lease of the house and shops in the Minster Yard should go to Roger's son, Anthony Jackman.

[35] See Appendix 5.
[36] McKerrow, op. cit. (note 2).
[37] T. Baker, *History of the College of St. John the Evangelist, Cambridge*, ed. J. Mayor (Cambridge, 1869), i, p. 433, ll. 19–23; p. 443, ll. 31–33; p. 466, ll. 9–10.
[38] For William see T. Baker, op. cit. (note 37), i, p. 386, ll. 10–11; p. 400, ll. 9–10; p. 436, ll. 16–20.
[39] *IGI*: Jane Foster married Roger Jackman on 30 June 1605; Anthonye Jackman was christened 1 May 1606 and Margaret Jackman was christened 25 January 1608. Roger Jackman christened nine children between 1606 and 1621, four of whom died in infancy. The records are, however, incomplete: Margaret Foster's will names another Jackman child, Matthew, who is not among the nine children whose christenings appear in the parish records.

Jane Jackman is given 'a Coveringe of Arras worke and halfe a dosen of siluer spoones of the better sorte' as well as one of the best feather beds.

The main beneficiary of Anthony Foster's will, apart from his widow, was the John Foster whose inventory was made in 1616. The business John took over, although we do not know its value, must have been large and well established. The will disposes of legacies amounting to £131 10*s.* (including £18 in debts owing to him) but does not give any details of the value of his stock and binding tools or of his household goods and property. Anthony had two houses, one outside the liberties and another 'within'; the latter, the stationer's house, was occupied by his 'cosin' John Foster at the time the will was written. 'The vse and occupation of my shopp and all the wares bookes and other implements and working instruments' were bequeathed by Foster to his cousin John 'at the discretion of my wyfe during her life'. Anthony's will does not simply turn over his shop and stock to John, but instructs Margaret Foster to offer John preferential treatment as far as the business is concerned: 'I will that she deale better wth him therein then wth and other and that he have the same at an easie rate and better cheape then and other man so that he be helpinge and assistinge to her'. That John Foster was heir to Anthony's business is clear: as well as the use of the shop, goods and tools at 'cheape' rates in return for assistance to Margaret, John was to receive £40, by far the largest individual legacy in the will. John was not, however, given the leases outright, and the details of Margaret's will direct that when John Foster should die the property would not be his to dispose of as he wished. Margaret makes clear that she owned the leases of at least the stationer's shop and the 'three[?] builded Shoppes': 'my dwellinge house in the Minster yarde wth all shoppes and other houses and the Yard now impayled belonginge vnto it'. No mention of property outside the Minster Yard is made in Margaret's list of leases. The leases of the Minster Yard properties were given to John Foster only for use during his lifetime, after which they were to become the property of Anthony Jackman. Margaret directs that any attempt by John to circumvent the terms of his tenure will result in the revocation of the terms of the will:

And if it please god to call him [John Foster] out of this miserable Worlde before the Expira*ti*on of ye said yeares in the said lease conteyned then I giue the same lease for the yeares that shalle so endure after the liffe of the said John Foster to Anthonie Jackman sonne of Roger Jackman of the Cittie of Yorke Stacioner Item my will is that the said John Foster shall not surrender the said lease to defraude this bequest to the said Anthonie Jackman and if he doe or goe aboute the same then I will and my minde is that the same bequest of the lease aforenamed by me to him giuen shalbe vtterlie voide and of none effect And then I giue the same lease and all my right therein to Anthonie Jackman duringe the yeares therein to expire[40]

This clause may reflect Margaret's mistrust of John or be no more than careful provision for all eventualities. The lack of any mention of the book stock suggests that John Foster had already bought this from Margaret, presumably at preferential rates as instructed by Anthony. But it seems that, even if John had purchased the stock, he was still dependent on Margaret for cash. The first bequest in Margaret's will records his outstanding debt to her: 'I giue vnto My Cosen John Foster Twentie poundes w^{ch}

[40] Margaret Foster's will (see Appendix 5).

he oweth me as borrowed money wch I lent him and should haue beene repaid me long since'.

The exact family relationship between Anthony and John Foster is not clear. A John Foster, son of William, was christened on 22 August 1584 in the parish of St. Michael le Belfrey, and this may identify him as the son of Anthony's brother William, who at the time of Anthony's death was living in London.[41] Anthony appears to have had no surviving male children, and no records of christenings which name him as father have been found. That he did have married daughters, or near relatives whom he regarded as daughters, seems likely: the case for Jane Jackman as Anthony's daughter is outlined above. The similar level of provision in his and his wife's wills for the Brice family (Alice Brice, her children, her unborn child) and John Brice's nomination both as guardian of Anthony Marsh and as another of the 'supervisors' of Anthony's will suggest that the Fosters may have stood *in loco parentis* to Alice Brice. It is possible that John Brice was, like Roger Jackman, the Fosters' son-in-law. A marriage is recorded between John Brice and a Margaret Foster in 1609. If, as the Christian name suggests, she was the daughter of Anthony and Margaret, then her marriage to John Brice would have made her stepmother to John's surviving children (Mary and John) from a previous, untraced, marriage. Margaret cannot have lived long after marrying Brice, since by 1610 he was married to Alice. Although his relationship to the Fosters as son-in-law was cut short by Margaret's death, it seems that the couple continued to regard him as son-in-law, and to make the same provision for his children and new wife Alice as for the children of their surviving daughter, Jane Jackman. In the absence of a surviving son, Anthony looked to John Foster, his 'cosin', as his successor in business, and John's presence in the house in the liberties at the time of Anthony's death suggests that he was already working there (and had probably been trained by Anthony) as his assistant. Christened in 1584, John would have been in his mid-twenties when Anthony died, and it seems that he married soon after becoming his own master on the death of his uncle. In view of the detailed provision for family members in Anthony's will, it seems unlikely that he would have omitted his main heir's wife from the will entirely if John had already been married in 1610. John's marriage probably took place some time between Anthony's death in July 1610 and September of the following year (when John's first son, called Anthony after his benefactor, was christened). Margaret Foster's will names his wife as Joan, but no record of the marriage has been found. The christenings of four children of John Foster took place between 1611 and 1616 (Anthony, Alice, Judith, and John).[42] Margaret's will refers to another daughter of John's called Margaret, who is given £10. It seems that John Foster and his wife, like the Jackmans and the Marshes, marked their relationship with the elder Fosters by giving the names Margaret and Anthony to their first-born children.

---

[41] *IGI*: the christenings of two other John Fosters are recorded in other parishes, in 1606 and 1609. The christening of John, son of William, in 1584 is thus the only one which identifies a John Foster of roughly the right age.
[42] *IGI*: Anthony, christened 28 September 1611; John, 18 August 1616; Alice, 10 June 1613; Judith, 17 August 1615. All were christened in the parish of St. Michael le Belfrey.

John Foster's marriage and philoprogenitive energy undoubtedly explains why he needed to find further property in the Minster Yard. From 1611 he paid yearly rent of 6s. 8d. for 'a little house next adjoyninge to m^r Swinburns hous, And for one little house next adjoyninge or under the Chapter hous'.[43] At the time of his death he was also renting a house in Jewbury, outside the city walls, where he kept 'two kyne and hay' along with other 'implements'.[44]

What happened to John Foster's book stock and who rented the stationer's shop after his death are not known. The Chamberlain's Rolls are patchily preserved after 1620 and John Foster, 'deceased', was still being named as renting the Minster Yard property as late as 1628. Then in 1633/34 'Joan Bennet widowe' is named as paying the half-year's rent for the stationer's shop and, for the first time, the 'three[?] builded Shoppes' are treated separately, being devised to Lowrence Watterworth (probably a relative of Tomisin, one of John Foster's debtors).[45] As John Foster's wife was named Joan it may be that she kept on the business, remarried, and was widowed, but there are no other Bennets known in the York book trade at this time, and Margaret Foster's will had very specifically said that on John Foster's death the leases should go to Anthony Jackman, who would have been about twenty-eight by 1634. There is, however, no evidence that Anthony Jackman ever occupied the shop or took up the business, and ten years later the occupant of the shop was Mark Foster, whose inventory of 1644 survives.[46]

The relationship between Mark Foster and his predecessors Anthony and John is not at all clear, and it seems likely that Mark Foster belonged either to a distant branch of the family or, perhaps, to a different family altogether. Mark Foster, son of Richard, was christened in St. Michael le Belfrey in 1617, and a Richard Foster was noted above (p. 2 with note 9) as trading as a stationer with the city council's permission between 1608 and 1610. (The family tree of Richard and Mark Foster (Table 2) traces three generations of the family.) In 1609 and 1610/11 Richard was living in the parish of St. Michael le Belfrey.[47] Although Anthony Foster is known to have had a brother Richard, it is unlikely that this is the same man since, according to Margaret's will of 1613, her brother-in-law was then living miles from York, in

---

[43] YML, Chamberlain's Rolls, E.1/115–23. The wording quoted above is from E.1/118. In some entries the second 'little house' becomes a 'little garthinge or yard'. This may be the lease of one 'Stable' partly in 'Willm Blanchard yard' and the 'stable baye' worth £2 given in the list of Foster's leases (see p. 50, in Appendix 1).

[44] Davies, op. cit. (note 1), p. 373.

[45] YML, Chamberlain's Rolls, E.1/134.2. John Foster's name recurs in the second half of 1634 (E.1/136), and the last two rolls, for 1678 and 1678/79, are too late to be of any help. For Tomisin Watterworth (whose father was named Lowrence) see Appendix 3.

[46] Mark Foster's inventory is printed in R. Welford, 'Booksellers' stock, seventeenth century', *Notes and Queries*, 9th series, 2 (1898), 45. Its source is a copy found amongst the MSS of Canon Raine. Administration of Mark Foster's estate was granted, 22 December 1644, to Thomas Bambrough of York, yeoman.

[47] *IGI*: Mark Foster, son of Richard, was christened on 27 April 1617. For Richard Foster see note 9 above. Richard Foster was assessed at 9d. (21 June 1609) and 3d. (31 January 1611) by the parish authorities (Borthwick Institute of Historical Research (henceforth BHI), PR.Y/MB.33, St. Michael le Belfrey, York, Churchwardens' Assessments and Accounts, vol. ı [31 January 1610/11], [unfoliated]).

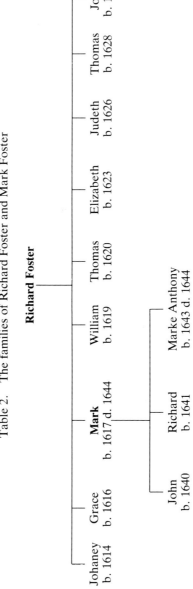

Table 2.   The families of Richard Foster and Mark Foster

Stainforth. The Richard who is recorded as a York stationer seems to have been in York throughout this period, christening and burying children from 1613 to 1616 in the parish of Holy Trinity, Goodramgate, and from 1617 until 1628 in the neighbouring parish of St. Michael le Belfrey. None of these children has the same name as any of the four children of Anthony's brother Richard, who are named in both Anthony's and Margaret's wills.[48] Neither will refers to a Richard Foster of York, stationer. If the York Richard was a relative, he was not close enough (despite his physical proximity) to be a beneficiary. Nothing else is known of Richard Foster the stationer, beyond his publication of a book from an address near the Minster gates.[49] This, then, is the father of the Mark Foster whose stock was inventoried in 1644.

The stock of Mark Foster was valued in what seems to have been the stationer's shop. The inventory made in 1644 describes his shop as 'under the shadow of the Minster', and one item in the inventory of his goods mentions 'five short end shelves next the Minster doore'. This sounds very like the stationer's shop on the west side of the south door, though it could conceivably refer to the first of the small shops to the east, which might explain why its value was so much smaller than that of John Foster's stock. Another reason for the low value of the stock may have been Mark Foster's age: christened in 1617, he was about twenty-seven when he died, giving him too short a period to acquire a large stock. What happened to the stock and shop after Mark's death is unknown. Three years before he died, Mark had christened a son called Richard. This may be the same Richard whose name appears in an imprint of 1659, dwelling in the Minster Yard.[50] Thus there were Fosters selling books in the Minster Yard for about eighty years; but how the family of Anthony and John connected with that of Richard, Mark, and the later Richard — if, indeed, there was a connection at all — remains unknown.

Almost all the records of christenings and marriages relating to the Fosters are from the parish of St. Michael le Belfrey, which lies close to the Minster and which served as parish church for those who lived within the Minster liberties. There were, of course, other families of the same name in other parishes, and the family of Richard Foster, which apparently moved there from the next parish in Goodramgate in about 1616, has been noted above (pp. 13 and 15 with note 48). However, the recurrent Christian names in the evidence about family relationships provided by wills and parish records (some certain, some tentative) point to a core of family members resident here from the 1570s until the 1640s, and perhaps beyond. Several of them were buried in the 'high quire' of St. Michael's: Anthony Foster in 1610; John's first child Anthony, who died in 1612 before he was six months old; Margaret, Anthony's wife, who died in 1613; John Foster himself in November 1616; and Mark Foster, whose 1644 inventory

[48] *IGI*: Richard Foster of York christened children called Johany, Grace (Holy Trinity, Goodramgate); Mark, William, Thomas, Elizabeth, Judeth, Thomas, and Joan (St. Michael le Belfrey). Richard Foster of Stainforth, Anthony's brother, had four daughters: Ellen, Ann, Isobell, and Brigett.
[49] Richard appears in the imprint of *STC* 6441 (see note 20 above). Since Anthony Foster's will mentions two brothers in London (William and John), it is possible that the York family was connected with the Richard Foster, bookseller, working in Fleet Street in 1549 (Plomer, op. cit. (note 2)).
[50] For Mark's children see note 49. The second Richard Foster of York appears in the imprint of Wing R1035, *The Rendezvous of General Monck* (York, 1659).

survives, was buried there on the same day as his infant son Marke Anthony (and the unusual combination of names, one from each of the two Foster families distinguished above, adds another hint of a relationship between the two).[51] As booksellers and bookbinders the successive Fosters all worked within the Minster Yard and lived either in the yard or in the parish of St. Michael le Belfrey. Like Anthony Foster, other members of the trade, his associates, and John Foster's debtors also had houses in the parish of St. Michael le Belfrey. Assessments were made by the parish officers in 1609 and 1611 on Foster's widow, and on Roger Jackman, Thomas Gubbin, and Richard Foster from the book trade; on John Bousfield, one of John Foster's appraisers; and on four of his debtors, Sir Edward Stanhope, John Standeven, Thomas Millington, and Tristram Britton.[52]

Buyers of Books in York and Foster's Debtors

One obvious customer for a shop situated so close to it was the Minster itself. John's predecessor Anthony Foster is recorded as selling books to the Minster chapter between 1580 and 1607, and clearly the shop was well placed to develop a regular trade of this kind. The Fabric Rolls of the Minster record payments to Anthony Foster for quires of paper, for binding paper into music books for the choir, and for psalters, psalms, and communion books, a trade continued by his 'cosin' — in 1611/12 John was paid £2 16s. for a new bible 'for the quier' and 8s. for two service books for 'Mr Tucker & Mr Fox'.[53] Claire Cross points out that the Reformation had brought about a reduction in the numbers of Minster clergy which persisted throughout the second half of the sixteenth century (emptying former ecclesiastical buildings, which subsequently became dilapidated or were roughly converted). The prebends were highly educated men, and their wills indicate an increase in their ownership of humanist books, but for the most part they were not resident. The vicars choral, who were resident and who worked in the Minster, were locally educated men with a conservative tendency who, on the evidence of their wills in the sixteenth century, owned relatively few books. Claire Cross points to a wide gulf, in terms of education and book ownership, separating the prebends and the vicars.[54] As well as the Minster clergy,

---

[51] F. Collins (ed.), op. cit. (note 8), pp. 117, 118, 123, 132, 215, 218. Mark Foster had three sons: John, christened 25 July 1640; Richard, christened 16 September 1641; and Marke Anthony, christened 7 October 1643. All were christened at St. Michael le Belfrey.

[52] Two records of parish assessments survive for this period in BHI, PR.Y/MB.33, St. Michael le Belfrey, York, Churchwardens' Assessments and Accounts, vol. I [31 January 1610/11], 21 June 1609 [unfoliated]. They give assessments varying from 3d. for Richard Foster to 4s. for Stanhope. The widow Foster was assessed at 8d.

[53] YML, Fabric Rolls, E.3/57, 58–59, 61, 62.1–2.

[54] C. Cross (ed.), op. cit. (note 30), pp. iv–x. For the state of the city's buildings see J. C. H. Aveling, *Catholic Recusancy in the City of York 1558–1791*, Catholic Record Society Publications, Monograph Series volume 2 (London, 1970), p. 5.

Table 3.   John Foster's debtors: analytical table

Name	Reference Number in Appendix 3	Profession or Title	Resident	Dates	Education	Debts
A. Clergy						
(i) York						£. s. d.
R. Leake	(10)	?Prebend	?York	*fl.* 1589–1642	C (St. Cats.)	1 4 2
?Mr. Sadler	(29)	Rector	York	*fl.* 1605–?	?	4 7
W. Cockson	(30)	Rector	York	*fl.* 1584–1631	?	2 2
?T. Hingston	(35)	Vicar Choral	York	*fl.* 1590–1620	?	1 0
M. Dodsworth	(38)	Chancellor	York	*fl.* 1565–1628	C (St. John's)	4 8
?R. Bellwood	(43)	Vicar	York	*fl.* 1598–1623	C (Trinity)	1 6 0
(ii) Country						
M. Dunwell	(1)	Vicar	Collingham	*fl.* 1618–61	?	4 9
T. Squire	(9)	Vicar	Escrick	*fl.* 1609–63	C (Christ's)	1 14 9
W. Jagure	(11)	Vicar	Kirkby c. B.	*fl.* 1592–1627	?	2 3 10
?R. Firbank	(12)	Vicar	Thirkleby	*fl.* 1551–1624	C (Trinity)	5 6
R. Bubwith	(16)	Rector	Ackworth and Rothwell	*fl.* 1584–1627	C (St. John's)	13 6
A. Cooke	(17)	Vicar	Leeds	1564–1632	O (B'nose)	8 0
H. Smith	(18)	Vicar/Rector	Hemsworth	*fl.* 1587–1615	C (Trinity)	5 4
W. Greene	(22)	?Vicar	Heslington	*fl.* 1579–1640	C (Clare)	8
H. Bankes	(28)	Rector	Settringham	*fl.* 1581–1633	C (Christ's)	8 0
E. Walker	(33)	Vicar	Stillingfleet	*fl.* 1583–1617	?	4 0
J. Smyth	(34)	Vicar	Calverley	*fl.* 1607–28	C (Clare)	1 0 0
T. Leng	(37)	Vicar	Strensall	*fl.* 1606–31	?	6
?W. Sanderson	(41)	Rector	Thorpe B.	*fl.* 1605–26	?	1 0
B. Laity						
(i) Professional and Gentry						
Mr. Wilson	(4)	Attorney	?York	?	?	4 0
R. Claphamson	(5)	Notary	York	*fl.* 1610–35	?	1 4 6
T. Millington	(8)	Gentleman	York	d. 1624	?	1 0
Sir E. Stanhope	(24)	High Sheriff	York and Kirby Wharfe	*fl.* 1615–46	?	4
T. or H. Sandwith	(26)	Deputy Keeper of King's Evidences	York	*fl.* 1613–25	?	5 2
C. Wade	(36)	Chamberlain	York	*fl.* 1618–?25	?	3
(ii) Merchants, Tradesmen, and Others						
E. Secker	(2)	Vintner	York	*fl.* 1602–14	patr.	13 6
P. Williamson	(13)	Saddler	York	*fl.* 1604–19	?	1 3
?T. Williamson	(14)	?Vintner	York	*fl.* 1619	patr.	2 7
J. Standeven	(21)	Vintner	York	*fl.* 1592–1623	patr.	2 0
?R. Walmsley	(27)	Merchant	York	?	freed	10 8
W. Smythson	(32)	Draper	York	*fl.* 1593–1618	patr.	3 4
G. Dickinson	(39)	Haberdasher Alderman	York	*fl.* 1609–33	?	3 11
T. Watterworth	(40)	Wife	York	1589–1643	?	3 0
T. Britton	(42)	Embroiderer	York	*fl.* 1588–1625	patr.	6
C. Unidentified						
G. Townson	(3)	?	?York	?	?	1 5 10
Mr. Staveley	(6)	?	?York	?	?	6
Mr. Slator	(7)	?	?York	?	?	1 6
Mr. Walter	(15)	?	?York	?	?	14 0
Mr. Greenwoode	(19)	?	?York	?	?	1 5 3
D. Bell	(20)	?	?York	?	?	1 1 0
Mr. Bankes	(23)	?	Horton	?	?	7 6
W. Best	(25)	?	?York	?	?	2 6
J. Watt	(31)	?	?Thearne	?	?	4 0

Note: Based on Appendices 1 and 3. No attempt has been made to order these identifications by age since the evidence does not allow of easy comparison. Under 'Education' 'C' and 'O' have been used to identify Oxford and Cambridge universities, and the manner of the tradesmen's emancipation, whether through the completion of an apprenticeship or by patrimony, is indicated where known. It is probable that the debtors described as 'Mr.' in the 'Unidentified' section were clergymen, mostly resident in York.

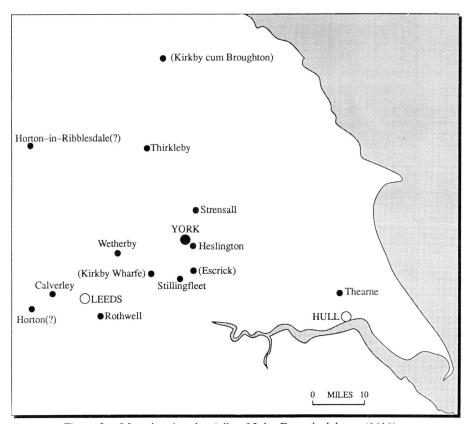

Figure 2.   Map showing domicile of John Foster's debtors (1616).
(Neither Leeds nor Hull nor the places named in parentheses are mentioned in the inventory.)

there were many city clergy in York, who provided another market for religious books.[55]

One known customer of the Foster shop from further afield, absent from the list of Foster's debtors (see Appendix 3), was Anthony Higgin, rector of Kirk Deighton near Wetherby from 1583, and subsequently master of St. Michael's Hospital at Well (1605) and dean of Ripon (1608).[56] 'Emptus Eboraci' appears in a number of his

[55] C. Cross (ed.), *York Clergy Wills 1520–1600: II City Clergy*, Borthwick Texts and Calendars, 15 (York, 1989). The distribution of the surviving wills and inventories printed by Claire Cross is, unfortunately, skewed towards the earlier part of the sixteenth century: only one will containing books belongs to the last quarter of the century, and the conservative bias of the books named in the earlier wills is unsurprising, given the fact that most of these clergy had been pre-Reformation priests. The absence of testamentary documents from late sixteenth-century York clergy means that it is impossible to judge how long the conservative tendency persisted among the city clergy.
[56] J. E. Mortimer, 'The library catalogue of Anthony Higgin, dean of Ripon (1608–1624)', *Proceedings of the Leeds Philosophical and Literary Society*, Literary and Historical Section, 10:1 (1962).

volumes surviving in Ripon Cathedral Library. A copy of Erasmus, *Enarratio in Psalmum xxxiii* (Basle, 1531), has the inscription 'Liber Anth. Higgin emptus a bibliopola Eboracensi, Forstero'; an 'Athanasii opera' (Basle, 1564) is inscribed 'Liber Anthonij Higgin emptus Eboraci maij 1585. 10sh.6d.'; and W. Vander Lindt, *Panoplia Evangelica* (Paris, 1564), has 'Anth: Higgin. pret. 2sh. 6d. Empt. Eboraci. 1589. Maij 24'.[57] All three books bought by Higgin in York are old books, and there is evidence of a second-hand trade in John Foster's inventory. As Mortimer remarks, 'a clergyman even in a small village like Kirk Deighton [Higgin's parish 1583–1605] had no need to be cut off from scholarly pursuits'. Her discussion of Higgin's catalogue suggests a widespread community of book-buyers, -lenders, -givers, and -exchangers among the Yorkshire clergy and gentry. Higgin's network of friends and colleagues covered a large geographical area, and the book-buying habits of this community suggest three circulation patterns for books: one of books obtained directly from booksellers principally in London, one of books bought locally in York, and one of the movement of books among collectors and authors by gifts and legacies. Considerable collections were built up by some local book owners. Dean Higgin had 758 books of theology in 1624. Alexander Cooke, vicar of Leeds and Puritan controversialist, whose *Pope Joan* was on sale in Foster's shop, owned a library which he valued at £100. The library of Tobie Matthew, archbishop of York, consisted at his death in 1628 of over 3,000 books, valued at £600.[58]

The list of Foster's debtors made on 26 November 1616 gives a partial idea of the social status of his clientele. A breakdown is given in the analytical table (Table 3). Of the forty-three names recorded by Foster's appraisers thirty-one can be identified with varying degrees of certainty.[59] In addition, the profession of 'Mr. Wilson', otherwise unidentified, is given as 'Attorney'. Since the list usually (but not always) notes where debtors outside York lived, it shows that Foster had customers in a thirty-mile radius round the city, reaching from Thirkleby in Cleveland to Thearne in Humberside, and possibly reaching up into Horton-in-Ribblesdale (see Figure 2).

Almost two thirds of Foster's identified debtors were clergymen.[60] Ten of these had livings outside York, and to their number should probably be added at least two further names, those of 'Mr Bankes of horton' and 'Mr John watt of Thearne'. Of the York clergy, four were attached to the Minster (Leake, Grene, Hingston, and Dodsworth), and three had city livings (Sadler, Cockson, Bellwood) all of which were close to the Minster (respectively Holy Trinity in Goodramgate, St. Crux, and St. Saviour's). Two others, Alexander Cooke, vicar of Leeds, and Henry Smith, vicar of Kellington, were chaplains to Edmond, Lord Sheffield, president of the king's Council

---

[57] J. E. Mortimer, op. cit. (note 56), 4, 21, 56. Mortimer's account is based on a contemporary catalogue of Higgin's divinity books: further information about Higgin's acquisition of books is to be found in those of his non-divinity books which survive in the Ripon Cathedral Library (on loan to Special Collections, Brotherton Library, University of Leeds).

[58] J. E. Mortimer, op. cit. (note 56), 4. For Cooke see Appendix 3; for Matthew see J. Raine, *Catalogue of the Printed Books in the Library of the Dean and Chapter of York* (York, 1896), pp. x–xi.

[59] For the evidence on which this section is based see Appendix 3.

[60] Davies (op. cit. (note 1), p. 36) misleadingly speculates on the importance of the county gentry and their families to Foster's trade.

of the North (1603–19), which was based in York. It is striking that out of the eleven clergymen who are recorded as taking a degree, only one, Alexander Cooke, graduated from Oxford. The remainder all went to Cambridge. Thomas Squire and Henry Bankes graduated from Christ's College, Robert Firbank and Henry Smith from Trinity, Richard Bubwith and Matthew Dodsworth from St. John's, James Smyth, William Grene, and Roger Bellwood from Clare, and Richard Leake from St. Catherine's. (Tobie Matthew, the archbishop, was an Oxford graduate, but his predecessor, Matthew Hutton, who died in 1606, attended Trinity College, Cambridge.) In age they ranged from their late twenties (Thomas Squire) to their late sixties (Matthew Dodsworth). The predominance of clergymen among Foster's debtors is a direct result of his shop's location in the Minster Yard in a city with a large number of clergymen within its walls and in the surrounding countryside.

Foster's other customers included gentry and city officials. Sir Edward Stanhope was sheriff of York in 1615; John Standeven, the recusant vintner, was chamberlain of York in 1594 and sheriff in 1608/09; Christopher Wade, gentleman, was successively chamberlain and sheriff in 1618–20; and George Dickinson, a draper with a substantial export trade, was a city alderman. Another official who was in Foster's debt was one of the two deputies, Thomas and Henry Sandwith, of Edward Bee, keeper of His Majesty's Evidences at St. Mary's Tower. Mr. Millington is probably to be identified with Thomas Millington, 'gentleman' of York, who died in 1623/24. The legal profession is represented by 'Mr Wilson Attorney' and by the public notary, Robert Claphamson, who was a witness and supervisor of the wills of both Anthony Foster (1610) and his wife Margaret (1613). Among the remaining debtors are several tradesmen, Peter Williamson a saddler (and perhaps his son Thomas, freed as a vintner in 1618), William Smythson a draper, and Tristram Britton an 'imbroderer'. If Robert Walmsley was related to the 'Rogerus Walmeslay, marchant' who became a freeman in 1568, he was also probably in trade. One woman, Tomisin Watterworth, is among Foster's debtors, owing him three shillings from 18 April 1613. She lived in the parish of St. Michael le Belfrey, and was married ten days before the appraisal was made.

Unfortunately there is no evidence of what Foster's customers bought from him, nor is it even certain that their debts were for books. The oldest of these good debts is that of Edmund Walker which dates back to October 1611, though the majority (twenty-seven out of forty-three) were incurred from 1614 to 1616. Even so, Foster seems to have allowed his customers generous credit.

The inventory made necessary by Foster's death gives only a snap-shot of his business in November 1616 and can give no firm indication of the relative importance of his various customers. Clergymen, however, appear to have been his most important customers among those allowed credit. Altogether nineteen clergymen owed Foster £11 3s. 6d. as compared to thirteen lay debtors owing £3 2s. 7d. The average debt of clergymen is c. 11s. 9d.; that of the laymen c. 5s. 8d. The debts of the clergy are biased towards those with country livings (£6 17s. 5d. as against £4 6s. 1d. for the city clergy). Yet, although the largest individual debt (£2 3s. 10d.), dated 16 May 1616, was incurred by William Jagger, vicar of Kirkby cum Broughton in

Cleveland, and two other country clergy, Thomas Squire of Escrick and James Smyth of Calverley, had debts between them of £2 14s. 10d., Richard Leake, prebend of York, owed Foster £1 4s. 2d., and from the city clergy Roger Bellwood owed £1 6s. The only layman in debt to Foster on a similar scale was the notary, Robert Claphamson (£1 4s. 6d.). It may be that Jagger, Squire, and Smyth were buying catechisms and instructional books for their parishes rather than books for their own study.

A limited number of the wills of Foster's debtors can be traced, but they tell little about his trade. Rather they show the kind of importance his customers attached to their books. Where the wills of four laymen customers make no reference to books (Claphamson, Millington, Smythson, and Wade), five out of the ten wills found for Foster's clergy debtors give books as legacies. In one case, William Cockson, rector of St. Crux, whose will makes no mention of books, is shown by his inventory to have had books worth £2 'In the Chamber w^{thin} the Studie Chambre'. Matthew Dunwell, vicar of Collingham, left his books to his son (his inventory does not mention books, but may be incomplete). Richard Bubwith, rector of Rothwell, gave one son-in-law Foxe's *Actes and Monuments*, divided two parts of Holinshed's *Chronicles* between his eldest son and a second son-in-law, and left the rest of his books to his second son, Samuel, who was to pay 'halfe value' for them. Edmund Walker, vicar of Stillingfleet, gave his cousin a 'Zuingli Bible' and a second book to another cousin. All of William Sanderson's books went to his son, along with his best gown and cloak. The largest collection of books in this group of clerics was owned by Alexander Cooke, vicar of Leeds, who owed Foster a modest 8s. He divided his books, which he valued at £100, between his two sons, and also divided his 'Paper Bookes' between them. He further specified that his nephew, Robert, at Oxford, was to receive his Rheims and Douai translations of the bible, and a Hebrew bible was left to a second nephew, also at Oxford. He also willed three works to his daughter, Elizabeth, including Foxe's *Actes and Monuments* and Paolo Sarpi's *Historie of the Councel of Trent*.[61] Cooke's library was unusually large, and most of his books, like those in Dean Higgin's library at Ripon, must have been bought from booksellers other than Foster or his predecessor. The books in Foster's inventory do include works in English and Latin which would have interested Cooke and other clergymen, and such customers no doubt encouraged the use of the devotional, instructional, and catechistical works Foster held in such quantity. But a substantial part of Foster's titles was aimed at a broader lay audience. The evidence of the list of debtors suggests that those buyers were mostly confined to the city. That, of course, may say more about the nature of Foster's trade than about the profile of the book-buying public in early Stuart Yorkshire.

---

[61] For Cooke's will and further discussion see J. Barnard, 'A Puritan controversialist and his books: the will of Alexander Cooke (1564–1632)', *The Papers of the Bibliographical Society of America*, 86 (1992), 82–86.

The Book-Stock Inventory[62]

The inventory of John Foster's shop and warehouse is long and detailed. As well as books it lists other wares sold in the shop and Foster's tools and equipment used in binding.[63] Many book titles appear more than once and, taking such duplication into account, there are about 750 individual titles in all. Not all of the books can be identified: some items give author's name and no title, and there are a few bundles of unidentifiable books (for example, 'sticht bookes litle works', 'ten other books in octavo'). In all, it is possible to distinguish 3,373 copies of books, worth £144 16s. 4d.[64] The printed books represent 88% of the total value of the inventory, which is £163 15s. 8d. Allowing for some failures of identification, it would seem that about 93% of Foster's books were printed in England, and about 7% imported from the continent. The relative cost of the continental books is, however, high: they represent almost 19% of the total *value* of the book stock, despite being only 7% of the volume of stock. Books in English predominate, and other modern European languages (French, Italian, and Spanish) are scantily represented. Books in languages other than English constitute roughly 20% of the stock. Of these, the Latin books account for the vast majority, and are almost entirely either continental books or Latin school-books printed in England. The few books in Greek and in Hebrew are mostly dictionaries and grammars, and law French is found amongst the legal books.

The lay-out of the inventory suggests that the valuers were working their way around the shelves, starting at the front of the shop with bound volumes and working their way back, through the books in quires, to the warehouse. The majority of Foster's books appear to have been bound or stitched, ready for sale. Foster was his own binder: the inventory includes stocks of skins, pasteboards, vellum, forrel, 'Clasps, Bosses, and Nayles', pressing- and backing-boards, and a composite lot of 'Workinge Tooles', itemized as 'Rowles, Riglittes, Presses with plough hammers, beating Stone, with two Paire of Mooles [moulds?] for Paistebordes, and all other Tooles belonging to the Trade'. These working tools are valued together at £6, and altogether the items associated with binding (tools and materials) are valued at £8 6s. 6d. (about 5% of the total value of the inventory). Foster also stocked blank paper which he bound up for sale as copy books and account books: his stock includes thirty-two 'Paper Bookes' in various sizes and bindings, from small copy books at 4d. each to a folio paper book with clasps at 3s. 4d. The valuers describe the paper books in detail: some are 'of Duch paper', one is ruled, two are bound in leather. The 'paper

---

[62] Appendix 1 gives a list of corrections and additions which need to be made to Davies's transcript of John Foster's inventory. The analysis which follows is derived from a database constructed from Davies's printed list merged with the corrections and addenda using 'Paradox' software. A disk of the database is available from the Institute of Bibliography and Textual Criticism, University of Leeds.

[63] Davies, op. cit. (note 1). For the purpose of the analysis 'the inventory' is taken to mean the inventory of the shop only, and therefore excludes the household goods listed by Davies separately, op. cit. (note 1), pp. 372–74.

[64] Both figures are minimum values. The occasional omission of a book's value, and the few items in the inventory where a number of copies is not specified, mean that both the count of copies and the overall value of books would in reality be slightly higher than the figures given here.

Table 4.* Relative values of the several kinds of book inventoried

Davies page	Description	Average price in old pence
342–44	in folio	111.8d
345–50	in quarto	37.1d
350–57	in octavo	13.0d
357	in Twelve, ph.	15.3d
357–58	in Twelve, plaine	8.7d
358–59	in 16, gilt & fillites	9.7d
359	in 16, plaine	11.4d
359–60	Lattin bookes in 16	11.5d
360	in 24	25.2d
360	in 32	5.6d
360	Writeinge Tables in sortes of 16	2.3d
360[addenda]	folio	22.7d
360[addenda]	quarto	6.3d
360	Sticht Schoole, octavo	2.3d
361	Sticht folio. Musick	30.9d
361	Song Bookes, quarto	38.2d
361–63	Sticht Bookes, quarto	2.8d
363–64	Sticht bookes, octavo	2.0d
364–65	folio queares	42.0d
365–66	quarto queares	13.9d
366[addenda]	folio	24.0d
366–68	octavo queares	2.8d
368	in twelve, queares	9.6d
368–69	in 16, queares	7.3d
369[addenda]	32°	6.0d
369	in the Wairehouse, folio	19.5d
369–70	quarto	5.2d
370–71	octavo	2.0d
370[addenda]	16°	1.2d

* In this and all subsequent tables, figures are rounded to one decimal place. Davies's page numbers are given, but items excluded in Davies's printed version are included here, marked 'addenda' (Appendix 1).

Note: This table excludes a few printed items, mostly single-sheet folios, which appear on p. 371 listed not as books but amongst the binding materials and the 'Paper of Sortes', some of them perhaps destined for use as waste paper.

booke of Ryall paper of five queares in forrell', the most expensive of them all at 7s. 6d., was perhaps a great ledger or account book. The paper stock is described in similar detail: one ream of ruled paper and eighteen quires of copy paper are specified, as well as quires of 'Gilt', 'Duch', 'Damaske', and 'Venice' papers. Foster's practice, judging from the paper books already in the shop, was to bind such books only one or two at a time, and to keep examples of each kind to show to customers.

Bookselling, particularly in provincial towns, was frequently combined with other retailing activities. The Foster business shows that York was a big enough centre to maintain a bookseller–binder in trade without recourse to sidelines such as pills and potions, grocery, or haberdashery. All of the non-book items listed at the end of the inventory have an obvious place in a stationer's shop: maps, pictures, ink, pen-sheaths, wax and seals, spectacles and spectacle-cases, boxes and bandboxes. The scales listed in the inventory may have been shop equipment rather than items intended for sale. Foster's stock of maps was not large: one map of Yorkshire (1*s.* 2*d.*) and twelve small maps, worth 9*s.* 8*d.* in all. The pictures, not individually described, include 'borders of Kings and others' (presumably wall decorations) at 8*d.* each, a group of six pictures at 4*d.* each, and another lot of twenty-four at 2*d.* each.[65] The other merchandise (ink, spectacles, etc.) has a total value of £4 13*s.* 4*d.*

The stock of books, on the other hand, is extensive. Starting with the more elaborate folio bibles, the valuers worked steadily through folios, quartos, octavos, books in twelve ('phillites' and plain) and in sixteen (gilt and fillets, and plain). Next came Latin books in small formats (16°, 24°, and 32°). Stitched books, including some music books, came next and account for about a quarter of the stock, followed by books in all formats in quires (another third of the stock) and, finally, books in the warehouse (about one twelfth). Table 4 uses the groupings of books as laid out in the inventory (principally by format and binding) to show the relative values of the different kinds of book as determined by the assessors. This gives an idea of the likely lay-out of the shop and the way in which, to those within the trade, books might be categorized. It is easier, perhaps, to grasp the size and proportions of Foster's stock by using less elaborate descriptions. Table 5 below shows the proportions of stock arranged simply by format. Percentages of stock are given both for the quantities of books of each format which constituted Foster's entire stock, and for the value of the stock as distributed between the books of different formats. The information from

Table 5.   Format of books: quantity and value

Format	Quantity	Value
2	4.4%	30.1%
4	19.5%	30.0%
8	60.8%	29.3%
12	2.7%	2.6%
16	7.8%	5.7%
24	0.3%	0.8%
32	1.5%	0.9%
s.sh. fol.	3.0%	0.2%
not known	0.1%	0.4%

which this table is compiled is necessarily incomplete. In some cases, although we have information about the format and the value of an entry in the inventory, no quantity is given. Consequently, the apparent discrepancy between quantity and value (in cases

[65] The pictures are all together valued at 6*s.* 8*d.*

where the percentage of value is higher than the percentage of copies) may in part be attributable to incomplete information on quantity. Such cases are few, however, and are unlikely to be more than marginally significant. In Table 5 the relative value of the folio books is at once apparent: folios, which make up 4.4% of the stock, are worth over 30% of the total value. Conversely the octavo books, the most common format in terms of volume, are relatively cheap. The smaller formats are of little importance here: the bulk of the stock, in terms of value, is split almost evenly between folio, quarto, and octavo books.

1. Subject Categories

The subject breakdown of Foster's stock reflects what is known about early seventeenth-century York. During Elizabeth's reign York had prospered and grown. A revival in trade, in population levels, and in numbers of resident gentry is observable from the 1560s onwards. York had six major church courts as well as

Table 6. Foster's entire stock by subject category

Subject	% of copies	% of value
Religion (inc. sermons)	16.7%	25.3%
Bibles/service books	6.3%	19.8%
School-books[1]	18.9%	27.8%
Law	5.7%	2.2%
Science	4.8%	1.3%
Info/instruction (inc. music)	2.0%	3.9%
Modern literature	2.1%	2.4%
History	0.7%	2.0%
Prayer-books	2.3%	
Geography/travel	0.2%	1.3%
Verse	1.3%	1.4%
Politics	1.5%	1.1%
Catechisms[2]	3.5%	0.7%
Miscellaneous	20.3%	3.9%
Not known	11.8%	7.6%
	100.0%	100.1%

[1] Includes university texts as well as elementary and grammar-school books.
[2] Some catechisms (e.g., Nowell's) are counted not here, but in the 'School-books' category.

secular courts, and the educational provision within the city was growing: after 1575 there were two grammar schools and probably a petty school in each parish. Increasingly, boys from York were going on to Cambridge or the Inns of Court. Palliser suggests that by 1600 the adult literacy rate may have been as high as 50%.[66] John Foster's business was operating in the context of a growing (and increasingly lay)

[66] Palliser, op. cit. (note 4), c. 10 *passim* (prosperity); p. 174 (literacy).

3

market for books. In turning to an analysis of his stock in terms of the subjects represented, however, it must be recognized that the inventory lists *unsold* books, and such analysis can properly be used only as evidence of Foster's expectations about his market, rather than as evidence of what his customers actually bought. Which of these books remained unsold because Foster had misjudged the market, and which of them were titles which were turned over rapidly in his day-to-day trade are matters for speculation, not of verifiable fact. Table 6 gives the breakdown of Foster's entire stock by subject category. A remarkable feature of Foster's stock is the number of books which were *not* either religious or educational. The proportions of subject areas covered by Foster's stock become clearer if the above listing is simplified further. In Table 7 the subject categories are amalgamated into three main groups. Foster's stock,

Table 7.   Foster's entire stock in three main groupings

Subject group	% of copies	% of value
Religion (inc. bibles/service books/catechisms/ prayer-books)	28.8%	47.1%
School-books	27.8%	18.9%
All others (law/verse/geog/ politics/science/info/ lit/hist/misc)	31.6%	26.5%
Not known	11.8%	7.6%
	100.0%	100.1%

in terms of numbers of copies, thus falls neatly into thirds, with about thirty per cent each of religious, school and 'other', miscellaneous, books. (In this respect Foster's inventory is unusual in comparison with other provincial booksellers' inventories of the period, a point to which we shall return.) In terms of the *value* of the books, however, the picture is different: as far as investment of capital in stock is concerned, the religious books represent nearly half of Foster's assets, with 'others' — some specialist (law, science) and some popular and leisure reading — worth a quarter of the total value of the stock. School-books, while no doubt good sellers, represented less capital outlay. There is no direct information about Foster's sources of supply, and the absence in the inventory of any record of Foster's debts to the London trade is surprising.

   A picture of the relative cost of certain types of book can be offered in more detail by calculating the average price per copy for each kind of book. In some cases such an average price may not be typical: the geography/travel category, for example, has only 8 books — too small a sample to enable wider generalizations to be made. In most categories, however, Foster's holdings were much larger, with more than 50 books. The material stocked in large quantities is not surprising: Foster had 604 almanacs, all octavo, of which 550 were in quires and 54 were stitched (included in the miscellaneous category); and 180 octavo ABCs, of which 80 were stitched. The valuers made no distinction between the stitched and unstitched copies: almanacs are valued consistently at slightly less than 1.5*d* each, and ABCs at a halfpenny each. The only other item held in such great quantity was the *Degrees of Marriages*, a single sheet of which Foster had 100, valued at 24*d*. in all (fractionally less than a farthing each). Table 8 gives the average price per copy for each category of book, and shows the actual numbers of copies involved so that possible distortions caused by the size of the sample are obvious.

Table 8. Average price of books per copy for each subject category

Subject	No. of copies	Average copy price
Geography/travel	8	54.3d
Science	44	38.0d
Bibles/service books	213	32.4d
Law	74	27.0d
History	25	27.0d
Information/instruction	68	19.8d
(includes music	18	35.3d)
Religion	564	15.6d
(includes sermons	71	8.7d)
Literature	69	11.9d
Verse	42	11.9d
Politics	50	7.4d
School-books	938	7.0d
Prayer-books	76	5.9d
Miscellaneous	685	2.0d
Catechisms	118	2.1d
Not known	399	6.6d

The subject and price analysis of Foster's inventory (in Tables 6–8) allows some insights into the nature of his trade. The high incidence of religious books and of school-books is unsurprising. However, his stock of bibles and service books is notably extensive: psalters, psalms, and testaments feature in a wide variety of formats and bindings, from the elaborate bible 'in small folio roman with Com bost & buft' at 17*s*. 6*d*. to plain 'single Testaments in 16' at 9*d*. each. The disparity between subjects as proportions of stock and of value (see Table 6) is particularly marked in this case, where 213 books (only 6% of the total stock) are worth almost 20% of the total value. Foster clearly sold them to a wide variety of individual customers, a number of them wealthy, as well as supplying elaborately bound copies of bibles and service books to York Minster and no doubt to other religious institutions.[67] In this sector of his

[67] Some of the clergy among Foster's debtors (see Appendix 3) may have been buying books for presentation to, or on behalf of, their church libraries. See, for example, T. W. Hanson, 'Halifax parish church under the Commonwealth (John Brearcliffe, the antiquary: Part III)', *Halifax Antiquarian Society: Papers and Reports* (1909), 288–98, for evidence on parish libraries at this time. They may also have been buying catechisms, school-books, and psalms for their parishioners.

business, where the book became a luxury or semi-luxury product, Foster's twin trades as bookseller and bookbinder came together most profitably.

Bibles and service books were not, however, the only expensive books stocked by Foster. The number and value of the law books, which represent about a fifth of the overall value of the third category ('All others') in Table 7, are a reminder of the constituency created by York's civil and ecclesiastical courts, represented among Foster's debtors by the public notary, Robert Claphamson. Books of geography and travel, science and history, although low in number, have also a high average price. In the case of the science books, this must be in part because many of them — almost half — were continental books.

The most unusual aspect of Foster's stock, however, is the quantity of books in English accessible both to the professional and the non-professional secular reader as recreational reading.[68] Provision for the 'godly' reader is to be expected: among the books categorized as 'religious' there is a wide selection of vernacular works, from intellectually demanding theological exposition and Anglican polemic to relatively inexpensive devotional works, books of comfort and advice, and cheap collections of sermons. But what is particularly striking is the quantity of secular vernacular books, suggestive of a leisure readership across a wide social range. For the wealthier and more educated book buyer there are expensive folio editions not only of books recently translated into English (such as Holland's translations of Plutarch and Pliny, Florio's translation of Montaigne, and Yong's translation of Montemayor) but also of new English works (notably a bound copy of Jonson's folio *Workes* published the same year that the inventory was made, and an unbound folio edition (now lost) of Drayton's *Poly-Olbion*).[69] Also expensive were the music books, of which Foster had eighteen, including works by Weelkes, Youll, Allison, and Este, all dated after 1597.[70] The inclusion in Foster's stock of these literary and musical books at the expensive end of the market suggests that Yorkshire book buyers participated in the high culture of London and the court.

But not all the books which might be classified as vernacular leisure reading were as expensive as these. The *average* price of the books categorized as 'literature' and 'verse' (11.9*d*. in each case) shows that the folios were exceptional in their cost and that poetry, plays, and fiction were potentially accessible to a much wider audience than were expensive folios. These two categories include many recent vernacular works of poetry, fiction, and drama (for example, by Greene, Marlowe, Shakespeare, Wither, Lindsay, Mere, Daniel, Grymeston, Peacham, and Pettie), and a group of 'Twenty-seaven Play bookes, of sortes' worth 4*d*. each. Also among Foster's books are

---

[68] The discussion which follows is based on the identified books in the inventory, which are listed by author in Appendix 2. In most cases we here give name of author only, and the reader may refer to Appendix 2 for further details.

[69] *STC* records only the pirated folio of 1620. Another possibly lost edition in this category is Greene's *The Pleasant and Delightful History of Doraustus and Faunia*, listed as 'Dorastus and Favina'. Davies identifies this as a quarto of 1607, but *STC* has no record of this title before *c*. 1635 (*STC* 12291.5), where it is given as another edition of *Pandosto*.

[70] The unidentified sets of 'Ittallian Songes', 'Gombartes', and 'Courtmantians' may well be continental publications.

popular works such as *The Hystorie of the Seven Wise Maisters of Rome*, Johnson's *The Most Famous History of the Seuen Champions of Christendome*, Armin's *Cobler of Caunterburie*, Ford's *Famous History of Montelion*, Fletcher's *Nine English Worthies*, and King's *Halfe-penny-worth of Wit*. In terms of the whole stock, these books are a small proportion (3.4% of all copies) and are of no great value (3.8% of the value of the entire inventory) but they indicate, when taken together with the other vernacular works (books of instruction and information, history, politics, topical events, and the large number of ballads, prognostications, and almanacs), that the bookshop by the Minster door could meet customers' recreational as well as professional and educational needs. The whole range of vernacular poetry, music, drama, and fiction represented in Foster's inventory indicates, too, that Yorkshire readers were part of an established national audience for a specifically English, as opposed to a continental or neo-Latin, culture.

One other class of books represented in the inventory deserving attention is found among the religious books and has a specifically local dimension. This is a group of books by anti-Catholic polemicists patronized by the archbishop of York, Tobie Matthew, who had been appointed in 1606 for his vigour in pursuing recusants. The transition from Catholicism to Protestantism was slower in York than in Hull or Newcastle, and it was not until after the accession of James I in 1603 that the city corporation began subsidizing city livings in order to attract energetic and able ministers.[71] Archbishop Matthew gave active support to a violent pamphlet campaign against the Catholics. Of the eight polemicists identified by John Raine as the 'controversial retainers' of Archbishop Matthew, five had copies of their works in Foster's shop.[72] These are Thomas Bell (two works), whose *The Hunting of the Romish Foxe* is dedicated to four members of 'Her Majesties Counsel in the North of England', emphasizing its local connections; Edmund Bunny, a prebend of York (two works in six copies); Alexander Cooke (one of Foster's debtors) whose *Pope Joane. A Dialogue between a Protestant and a Papist* was published in 1610 with a dedication to Tobie Matthew; Thomas Morton, son of a York mercer and eventually bishop of Durham (two works in four copies); and Matthew Sutcliffe (single copies of two works).[73] Although Foster's inventory contained anti-Catholic works by other writers, Tobie Matthew's support of all these men gave local vigour to the national pamphlet war. Matthew made his remarkable library at Bishopthorpe ('the largest

---

[71] C. Cross, op. cit. (note 55), p. xiii. See also J. C. H. Aveling, op. cit. (note 54), c. 3.

[72] J. Raine, op. cit. (note 58), p. viii. The three missing men are John Favour, vicar of Halifax; Robert Cooke, brother of Alexander; and Francis Bunny, brother of Edmund.

[73] One of Bunny's works listed in the inventory, *Of the Head-corner-stone*, of which Foster had five copies, is not a polemical work but a substantial biblical commentary. The other work by Bunny was his Protestant adaptation of *A Booke of Christian Exercise* by the Catholic apologist Robert Parson. The first known edition of Parson's work dates from 1582 and it was frequently reprinted at Rouen or St. Omer. Bunny's version, first published in 1585, was frequently reprinted (seventeen editions in two years) and was itself immediately answered by Parson in an enlarged version of his own book (see *STC* 19354.1). Cooke was assisted by Matthew who intervened to secure his collation to the vicarage of Leeds in 1615, despite Cooke's refusal to subscribe to the articles of Canon xxxvi (R. A. Marchant, *The Church under the Law: justice and administration in the Diocese of York 1560–1640* (Cambridge, 1969), pp. 32–33).

private library in England at the time') available to other writers and preachers, regarding it as a 'theological arsenal' for attacking his enemy.[74] As bookseller, Foster helped to disseminate these texts, printed in London but locally written, as part of Matthew's sustained campaign against Catholicism in the north of England. Whether they obtained them from Foster or not, Dean Higgin and the York lawyer Sir Edward Stanhope (d. 1608) had anti-Catholic works by Matthew Sutcliffe and Thomas Morton, and both possessed Morton's *Apologiae Catholicae* (1605–06).[75]

To fulfil its practical function as an 'arsenal' of texts for use in pamphlets and sermons, Matthew's library had to contain the works of the enemy. His library therefore included a collection of forbidden Catholic books.[76] So too did Dean Higgin's library at Ripon and, more unexpectedly, so did Foster's stock. Bellarmine, one of the main targets of English anti-Catholic writers, is represented in the inventory by two copies of an unidentified 'Epetomij', valued at 13s. and almost certainly continental in origin. Other Catholic books in Foster's shop include a copy of Buckland's *Seaven Sparkes of the Enkindled Soule* (a recusant book printed on an English secret press); St. Francis de Sale's *An Introduction to a Devoute Life* (either Walter Burre's expurgated edition of 1616 or one of three Catholic editions published at Rouen and Douai in 1613 and 1614); and a single copy of Thomas à Kempis's 'Imitation, the fourth part' (printed at St. Omer in 1613, or possibly an English secret press edition of 1615).[77] A number of unidentified entries in the inventory may also be Catholic books: 'Pomerius de Beata Virgina [*sic* in Davies]' and 'Rerum Societatae Jesu [*sic* in Davies]', which occur together in the inventory, 'Rosary of Prayers', and 'Ignatius Instruction' could all be Catholic titles. Foster also stocked a book which, while not Catholic, was a proscribed work: Darrell's *A True Narrative of the Strange and Grevous Vexation of the Devil, of 7. Persons in Lancashire*. Darrell, an 'exorcist', was pronounced an impostor, degraded, and committed to the Gatehouse after being

---

[74] J. B. Gavin, 'Elizabethan bishop of Durham: Tobias Matthew, 1595–1606', Ph.D. thesis (McGill University, 1972), (copy deposited at YML), p. i. Gavin gives over chapter 5 to the library but Bernard Barr, 'The Minster library', in *A History of York Minster*, ed. G. E. Aylmer and R. Cant (Oxford, 1977), pp. 500–02, gives a brief and clearer sense of its extent and subject range. Matthew had at least ten works by Sutcliffe and Bell (Gavin, op. cit. (note 74), p. 303).

[75] J. E. Mortimer, op. cit. (note 56) (Higgin had seven books by Morton and two by Sutcliffe); Stanhope's library is listed in R. J. Fehrenbach (ed.), *Private Libraries in Renaissance England*, vol. I (Binghamton, N.Y., 1992).

[76] Gavin, op. cit. (note 74), pp. 301–02. John Raine reported: 'There are some books in the Archbishop's library connected with this controversy which it would be treason for an ordinary person to possess, and there are some others which must have been taken from the book and vestment bags of seminary priests when they fell into the hands of the poursuivant' (op. cit. (note 58), p. viii). One other Catholic text in Foster's stock was *Youle in Yorke* (*STC* 26098.5), a broadsheet defence of the 'Yule rydyng' ceremony suppressed in 1572. The price (0.08d. each) and the place of the entry in the inventory suggest, however, that this was old stock being used as waste paper.

[77] Identification is uncertain, but 'the fourth part' suggests that this must be either 'B.F.''s version of Kempis's *Imitation*, called *The Following of Christ. Devided into Foure Bookes* (St. Omer, 1613) or the version published by an English secret press in 1615 with additional sections by St. Bernard and Pico della Mirandola, though Foster also stocked the Stationers' Company edition of Roger's version of the *Imitation* (London, 1605–13).

examined in Lambeth in 1599. His book was ordered to be burned in 1600, yet Foster's inventory has five copies.[78]

Censored books have, of course, an attraction for the bookseller, but anti-Catholic writers and preachers, such as the group surrounding Tobie Matthew, needed banned books for material, and the reading of Catholic books extended beyond the clergy. Lady Margaret Hoby, a serious Puritan resident in Yorkshire, records in her diary of 1599–1605 reading or hearing others read from such books on two occasions. It may also be the case that since York contained a hard core of recusants, including one of Foster's customers, John Standeven, the bookseller may have been prepared to sell to local Catholics and others of unorthodox interests under the cover of offering a service to Anglican clergy.[79] While Archbishop Matthew, Dean Higgin, or Alexander Cooke might be expected to have copies of Catholic books in their working libraries, the appearance of such books in Foster's stock, even on a small scale, might suggest a wider circulation in a city where the campaign against Catholicism was not an intellectual exercise but an attack on an existing community of recusants. Booksellers, as much as archbishops and deans, were likely to handle surreptitious or banned works, though with no impunity and for different reasons.

2. Prices

The question of what the prices given in the inventory *mean* is, as is usual with inventories of this kind, difficult to answer.[80] Two of the assessors were themselves stationers, and theirs is a professional valuation. None the less, the question whether these prices represent their view of cost, wholesale, or retail prices (perhaps with some discounting) remains problematic. Many titles appear both in the lists of bound books and in the lists of books in quires; but examination of the differentials between titles with both 'in quire' and bound prices reveals no clear pattern, and obviously the style of binding and the binding materials themselves may vary so much in individual cases as to obscure any obvious rule of thumb. More fruitful is an attempt to look at those books for which there is evidence of retail pricing from elsewhere.

Mirjam Foot's 'Some bookbinders' price lists of the seventeenth and eighteenth centuries' has proved particularly helpful: the list of 'Books as they are sold bound' issued by Thomas Downes *c.* 1620 and giving retail prices for both London and Dublin

[78] *Dictionary of National Biography*; *STC* 6288.
[79] *Diary of Lady Margaret Hoby 1599–1605*, ed. D. M. Meads (London, 1930). Margaret Hoby reports that she 'hard Mr Rhodes read of the princples of poperie out of one of their owne bookes' and herself read 'a popeshe booke' (p. 120). Her diary is interesting for its record of her reading: as well as Puritan works of theology and devotional texts, she read doctrinal controversy, 'popeshe' books, and pamphlets of news and scandal. The sources of her books are not explicit, but she made a number of visits to York as well as to London, and at least five of the authors she names and four of the specific book titles she mentions appear in John Foster's inventory. For Catholicism in York see J. C. H. Aveling, op. cit. (note 54).
[80] J. Barnard and M. Bell, 'The inventory of Henry Bynneman (1583): a preliminary survey', *Publishing History*, 29 (1991), 5–46, discusses this problem. See also A. N. L. Munby, 'Fragment of a booksellers [*sic*] day-book of 1622', *Book Collector*, 3 (1954), 302–06, for an interesting puzzle about the way in which booksellers recorded the value of sales. Munby's fragment has double columns of figures, one of which seems to record the actual retail price, but the meaning of the other remains obscure.

Table 9.   Comparison of Foster's prices with prices available from two other
published lists

Book	Foster	Downes: London	Downes: Dublin	Munby
bible in 8ᵗᵒ phill Claspes	84	–	–	–
bible in 8ᵗᵒ bb wᵗʰ services	86	84	102	88
Com & psalmes in folio	80	84	108	88
Com & psalmes in 4ᵗᵒ phill	48	48	60	–
Com & psalmes phil Claspes	30	32	40	36
Com & psalmes in 16	22	22	28	–
Testament and Psalmes in twelve [plain]	28	–	–	24
Com test & psalmes plaine, 8°	41	–	–	48
Aesop, Fables, 8°	6–8 (4*d*. quires)	7	10	–
Aphthonii sophistae Progymnasmata, 8°	4–12	12	16	4 (old)
Castalio, Dialogorum sacrorum libri quatuor, 8°	8	10	14	–
Cato*, Dionysius, 8°	3 (2.5*d*. quires)	3	4	–
Cicero, De officiis, 8°	10	12	16	–
Cicero, Sententiae, 8°	12	–	–	–
12°	–	12	16	–
16°	16	–	–	–
Cordier, Colloquiorum scholasticorum libri quatuor, 8°	5.7	4	4	–
Isocrates*, 8°	3.3	4	6	–
Nowell*, Alexander, Cattachismes, 8°	3–4	4	6	–
Ovid*, De tristibus, 8°	3.5	4	6	4
Ovid, Metamorphoses, 8°	10.8 (6*d*. quires)	12	16	–
Price, Gabriel, The laver of the heart	4	–	–	4
Primers, 16°	4	4	4	–
Rastell, John, The exposicions of the termes of the lawes of England	16	–	–	18
Saint German, Christopher, Doctor and Student, 8°	12	–	–	14
Sallustius, 8°	11	12	16	–
Seton, John, Dialectica, 8°	11 (8*d*. quires)	12	18	–
Spagnuoli, Baptista, Adolescentia, 8°	6 (5*d*. quires)	7	10	–
Sturmius*, Joannes, Epistle, 8°	3.4	4	4	–
Swetnam, Joseph, Araignment	4	–	–	4
Terentius	8 (8*d*. quires)	9	12	–
Vives, Joannes Ludovicus, 8°	3	4	6	–
paire of Christall Spectacles	6	–	–	6–8
paire of green glass [spectacles]	2.7	–	–	6
[paper booke] of two queares A peece in narrow folio	8	–	–	10

* books appearing as 'sticht schoole' in Foster inventory and 'small Schoole-bookes' in Foot's list.

Note: Many of these titles appear in the inventory in several lots each (e.g., Aesop six times); hence in some cases a range in price is given, (e.g., 6–8*d*.). The lower of the prices usually (but not invariably) is given for the later of two or more lots, or for odd single copies.

(Foot's Table 2) contains eighteen titles identified in the Foster inventory, as well as a few bibles and service books which are comparable in format and binding.[81] Munby's 'Fragment of a booksellers [*sic*] day-book of 1622' offers fourteen prices for comparison and, although Munby's bookseller remains anonymous, his business seems to be similar in kind to Foster's in that the fragment records sales of paper, ink, wax, spectacles, and spectacle-cases.[82] For comparison the titles appearing in the Foster, Downes, and Munby lists are tabulated opposite (Table 9). Despite the frequency of bibles and service books in all three lists, the variety of contents (testaments, psalters, psalms, etc.) and of combinations of binding descriptions ('bost and buft', fillets, clasps, 'ovills', gilt, gilt edge, plain) makes exact comparison difficult. Only those items whose descriptions are very closely matched and therefore comparable are shown here. Prices are given in pence throughout.

Prices in the Foster inventory seem thus to correspond more closely to London than to Dublin prices, and tend to be fractionally lower than London prices. The location of Foster's business in York is a critical factor in considering how the assessors reached their valuations. Downes's list is evidence of a consistent marking-up of Dublin prices to take account of transport costs. York, though more directly accessible from London, none the less was far enough away to make carriage an expense which the bookseller had to pass on to the customer through the retail price. Johnson observes from his familiarity with booksellers' bills that 'a London bookseller, when supplying a bookseller in the provinces and paying the carrier's charges, would bill the provincial bookseller at a price very little below the retail selling price in London'.[83] If, as the above table suggests, the inventory prices are close to London retail prices, then it seems that the assessors were working to London retail prices, but that — in the context of a York bookshop — these were trade prices, and their assessment is of the actual value of the stock in hand to anyone taking over the business, rather than its potential value if realized by selling the books on to customers.

Johnson's 'Notes on English retail book-prices, 1550–1640' has 36 titles identifiable (though sometimes rather tentatively) as those stocked by Foster, and offers some confirmation that Foster's prices were close to London retail prices.[84] However, comparison with Johnson's list is complicated by a number of factors which make the results less than conclusive. Although 36 titles seem to match those in Foster's inventory, often the prices in the two lists are not for the same thing: where Foster's is a bound book, Johnson's price is for an unbound one, or *vice versa*. Johnson's prices are gathered from 18 different sources, including documents relating to provincial booksellers and other inventories of booksellers (including one in Edinburgh), which compounds the problem still further. To use any of Johnson's prices with confidence would entail taking notice of the kind of source for each price, which would present too many variables to make sense of a limited overlap. All that can be offered (taking into

[81] M. Foot, 'Some bookbinders' price lists of the seventeenth and eighteenth centuries', in *Economics of the British Booktrade 1605–1939*, ed. R. Myers and M. Harris (Cambridge, 1985).
[82] Munby, op. cit. (note 80).
[83] F. R. Johnson, 'Notes on English retail book prices', *The Library*, 5th series, 5 (1950), 83–178.
[84] F. R. Johnson, op. cit. (note 83).

account likely differentials between bound and unbound books, but without allowing for the possible anomalies in Johnson's sources) is the impressionistic view that, of the 36 common titles, 24 (that is, two thirds) have prices which suggest that Foster's are close to standard London retail prices. Again, as with the Foot list, Foster's prices tend to be slightly lower where there is a difference: 9 of the remaining third look too low for retail prices, and only 3 look too high. Johnson offers broad support for the view that Foster's valuers were working with London retail prices in mind, which for them represented the York trade price.

3. Age and Origin of Stock

Most of the titles listed separately in the inventory can be positively identified. The vast majority of these (over 90%) are books printed in England. The discussion of Foster's stock which follows is based on an analysis of the identified books but necessarily excludes certain classes of titles of substantial importance. All the many bibles and service books, some school-books and editions of classical authors, and those books described only vaguely or by quantity in composite bundles cannot be identified individually and are unavoidably omitted from the following discussion of imprint dates. Nevertheless, the individually identified books form a substantial sample, in all about 75% of the 3,373 copies listed in the inventory.

Using this sample a profile of Foster's book stock, and in particular the likely age of the books available for sale in his shop, can be achieved by analysing dates of imprint. For each identified book, two dates have been recorded: the date of the earliest known edition (noted as 'first date') and the date of the latest edition which Foster could have stocked (that is, the nearest date to 1616, the date of the inventory, recorded as 'second date'). Where a title had appeared only in one extant edition by 1616, the same date has been recorded in both categories. Two profiles of Foster's stock can therefore be generated: one which assumes that Foster had the *earliest* known edition of all titles, based on the first-date information; and one which assumes that Foster had the *newest* possible editions of the titles he stocked, based on the second date. This shows the two possible extremes, and the (unobtainable) truth about the age of Foster's book stock must lie somewhere between the two. English books and continental books have been analysed separately, revealing their different profiles.

i. *STC* Books

Foster had a few copies of titles whose first-recorded *STC* editions are dated *after* 1616; his copies came, presumably, from lost editions, and all such copies have been counted in the '1600+' category. Post-dating by printers is in some cases likely and might account for the 26 copies (worth 1s. 9d.) identified in *STC* as printed in 1617; these, too, are counted in the totals for '1600+' editions. Table 10 sets out the two possible profiles of the stock, measured by quantity (first two columns) and by value (last two columns). It is immediately apparent that Foster's stock may have consisted almost entirely of current and recent books. At one extreme, more than a third of his books were printed after 1599, and almost two thirds dated from 1575 onwards. At the other, 90% were printed after 1599, with 97% from the period 1575–1616. Given the number of books from the English Stock (see below) and the large number of bibles, psalms, and service books not included in this calculation, his stock of English-printed books was predominantly up to date. When we turn to the value of the books, as determined by the assessors, the picture is broadly similar. As far as the value of the books is concerned, it is the recently printed (1600–16) stock which is the most significant, representing somewhere between 56% and 83% of the total value of the sample. Books produced after 1574 constitute between about 82% and 95% of the value of the *STC* books. On the basis of these profiles, then, the picture is that of a provincial bookseller with an up-to-date stock whose contacts with the London distributors were quick and efficient.

Table 10.   *STC* books by date: quantity and value

	Quantity		Value	
	1st date	2nd date	1st date	2nd date
pre-1575	37.0%	2.5%	18.1%	5.1%
1575–99	27.9%	6.9%	25.2%	11.0%
1600+	35.2%	90.6%	56.7%	83.9%

The names of individual London printers and publishers in the imprints of the identified books give no clue to the identity of Foster's London suppliers. What the imprints do indicate, however, is that a large part of his stock consisted of books controlled by the Stationers' Company. Taking together these books which name the Stationers' Company in the imprint and those books which are known to have been part of the English Stock at the time (though the company does not necessarily appear in the imprint), 39% of all Foster's English books are company stock. More specifically, if we narrow the focus to his most recent books (that is, those with a second date of 1600 or after), then 60% of his newest *STC* books were under the company's control. This offers clear evidence of the company's dominance of the provincial trade, though it must also be said that, while the English Stock books account for 60% of the recent books as measured in copies, they represent only 28% in terms of value.

ii. Continental Books

In addition to the books identified in *STC*, most of the continental books in Foster's inventory have been identified (sometimes hesitantly) and the details of first dates and second dates have been recorded in the same way.[85] The continental books can

---

[85] The identification of continental books has relied mainly on H. M. Adams, *Catalogue of Books Printed on the Continent of Europe, 1501–1600 in Cambridge Libraries*, 2 vols. (Cambridge, 1967), and the *British Library Catalogue*. E. S. Leedham-Green, *Books in Cambridge Inventories: book-lists from vice-chancellor's court probate inventories in the Tudor and Stuart periods*, 2 vols. (Cambridge, 1986), has proved invaluable in helping to identify some of the trickier items. While titles have been, on the whole, satisfactorily identified, the search for edition dates has not been exhaustive, and as a consequence the second-date information in particular might well be augmented and altered (though perhaps not very significantly) by further searching.

therefore be analysed to provide the two possible profiles at the extremes of oldest and newest editions. The sample is, however, much smaller in the case of continental books: there are dates for only about 130 copies. The smaller size of the sample and the speculative nature of some of the identifications make for greater uncertainty, but the results suggest a different kind of profile amongst the continental books from that provided by the *STC* items. The following table presents the continental books in terms of both profiles, by quantity (number of copies) and by value. The difference

Table 11.   Continental books by date: quantity and value

	Quantity		Value	
	1st date	2nd date	1st date	2nd date
pre–1575	67.2%	26.1%	50.7%	14.6%
1575–99	29.5%	47.1%	42.4%	50.7%
1600+	3.3%	26.8%	6.9%	34.7%

between the continental stock and the English books is at once apparent: a far smaller proportion of the continental books is new — at most, a little more than a quarter date from after 1599, and between a third and three quarters date from after 1574. Either the continental books were very slow-moving or, much more likely, many of the continental books were specialist works for the professionally educated élite like Dean Higgin. The English part of the stock was on the contrary up to date and catered to a market which both readily absorbed the staple books of the London presses produced annually (almanacs, ABCs, bibles, school-books) and was anxious for the latest books (news, religious controversy, new literary works, and English translations). But if the continental titles were older and fewer they were, as noted earlier, proportionately more valuable. Although they were only 7% of Foster's stock, their value was 19% of the whole inventory.

Foster's inventory makes no distinction between the continental and English books and, if the inventory mirrors the lay-out of the shop, there was no separate section of continental books. The inventory does, however, specify 'old' books occasionally, sometimes by title as 'godly garden wth psalms old' but more often more generally: 'Old Statutes sticht', 'old gramer', 'Old bookes in octavo'. The 'old' books so described are mostly grammars, dictionaries, law books, and bibles, and account for about 6% of the total stock, but only 3% of the total value of the stock. 'Old' statutes, bibles, and law books deserved attention because they retained commercial and intellectual value (an 'old bible bb' was, for example, worth 4s.) but most 'old' books (176 of 202 copies described as 'old') were treated as job lots worth relatively little: the 'Old bookes in octavo', for example, were priced at 10s. 10d. for 92 books, less than 1½d. each.

A Basis for Comparison?

In his survey of recent work on the provincial book trade, Paul Morgan points out that 'Above all, the book trade in a place must not be treated in isolation, but considered in relation to its neighbourhood and compared with similarly sized towns or districts whose book-trade histories have been published; if unpublished inventories of individual traders are discovered, they must be put alongside published lists of the same time'.[86] Moreover, he notes that particular titles are often common to several inventories, and urges the computerization of such inventories to facilitate comparison. It is beyond the scope of this enquiry to embark upon such a large-scale undertaking, but we have scrutinized the available inventories of provincial book-sellers, even though these are too scattered to lead to any convincing overall view. The variety of the inventories currently in print makes comparison difficult. Some inventories are very detailed, while others are largely uninformative about the books they record; volume and value of stock vary widely; populations and demographic features of towns for which published inventories exist seldom offer a good match as between particular inventories. Even if a few of these factors seem to offer a reasonable comparison, the chances are that the inventories are not close enough in time to make the comparison a reliable one. It is with these caveats in mind that we attempt a comparison of the Foster inventory with others.

Two kinds of comparison are possible: one which puts the Foster inventory in the context of other York inventories, both earlier and later; and one which looks to inventories from other provincial centres in the seventeenth century. The inventory of Neville Mores, dated 1538, offers information about the stock of a prosperous bookseller who, like Foster, had his shop close to York Minster. Mores's business, however, was operating almost eighty years earlier than Foster's, and in the different social and economic circumstances of York's period of economic stagnation. The 1644 inventory of Mark Foster, working from what had been Foster's shop but not necessarily his business, while unfortunately much less detailed than those of Mores and John Foster (books are not individually itemized and no titles are given), offers a view of the state of the York book trade almost thirty years after John Foster's death.[87]

Despite the difference in size of the three businesses, in terms of stock and total value, there are some obvious similarities (Table 12). All three men appear to have been operating solely as bookseller–binders, with no sidelines in other retail commodities. Books represent in each case 86–88% of the total value of the inventories, and in the case of the two Fosters, despite the obvious difference in the overall value of their businesses, the binding tools and materials represent more or less the same proportion of their assets. While the lack of detail in the 1644 inventory prevents us from taking this three-way comparison further, more can be said about the kinds of books listed in the 1538 and 1616 inventories. The variety of subjects stocked by John Foster has been discussed above (see Tables 6 and 7). Whereas Foster's stock consists

---

[86] P. Morgan, 'The provincial book trade before the end of the Licensing Act', in *Six Centuries of Provincial Book Trade in Britain*, ed. P. Isaac (Winchester, 1990), pp. 31–39.

[87] For Mores see Palliser and Selwyn, op. cit. (note 16); for Mark Foster, Welford, op. cit. (note 46).

of about 30% each of three main categories (religious and service books; school-books; and 'others' such as law, verse, geography, politics, science), Mores's stock is much less varied. A large proportion — about two thirds — of his stock consists of religious and service books (double the proportion in the 1616 inventory) while school-books account for only about 16% of his stock (as against Foster's 28%). Law is a more prominent feature of Mores's stock (about 9% as against Foster's mere 2%) but there is very little in the 1538 stock of *any* subjects other than those already mentioned. Palliser and Selwyn remark on the apparently narrow specialization, suggesting that Mores was catering almost entirely to clergy and ecclesiastical lawyers, and point to the lack of even devotional works popular with the laity.[88] The books in Mores's list are valued at an average of 6*d.* each, while Foster's 1616 stock has an average price per copy of 10*d.*

Table 12. Foster's inventory compared with other York inventories

	Mores 1538	John Foster 1616	Mark Foster 1644
value of inventory (as %)	£3 14*s.* 7*d.* (100%)	£163 15*s.* 8*d.* (100%)	£25 12*s.* 0*d.* (100%)
value of books (as %)	£3 3*s.* 10*d.* (86%)	£144 16*s.* 4*d.* (88%)	£22 0*s.* 0*d.* (86%)
binding tools (as %)	8*s.* 2*d.* (11%)	£8 6*s.* 6*d.* (5%)	£1 11*s.* 4*d.* (6%)

Peter Clark, in his study of book ownership in three Kentish towns, points to quite extensive collections of books among the county gentry by 1600, and makes a compelling case for the 1590s as the breakthrough decade for book ownership among non-professional townspeople.[89] While the list of Foster's debtors gives little information about the county gentry (the only one of the debtors in this category being Sir Edward Stanhope), it does point to customers among both the professional and more middling tradespeople of York. The rise in wealth, population, educational opportunity, and levels of lay literacy, all of which were features of York in the Elizabethan period, is exemplified in Foster's stock as compared with that of Neville Mores.

The lack of detail in the 1644 inventory frustrates any attempt to quantify the stock owned by Mark Foster. The valuers reported books only by the shelf-ful: five 'foreshelves' of which one carried folio books, one quarto, and three octavo, totalling £12; five 'short end shelves' with books worth £6 10*s.*; other bound books on '12 shorte shelves att the low end of the shop, being all old ones' worth £2; and other stitched books and printed papers worth £1 10*s.* The arrangement of the books is similar to that

[88] Palliser and Selwyn, op. cit. (note 16); but note that their remarks on Foster, based as they are on Davies, are not therefore entirely accurate.
[89] P. Clark, 'The ownership of books in England, 1560–1640: the example of some Kentish townsfolk', in *Schooling and Society: studies in the history of education*, ed. L. Stone (Baltimore and London, 1976).

in the 1616 inventory, but with apparently a separate section of 'old' or second-hand books. This seems like a sizeable stock — in which case, either the value of books had fallen or the stock was undervalued — but there is no information as to the numbers of books involved. A falling-off in trade at this time would not be surprising: in April the siege of York by Parliamentarian forces began, and the usual communications between city and countryside were disrupted. The perfunctory nature of the inventory, taken on 2 May in the early weeks of the siege, arises perhaps from the circumstances under which it was made, rather than any deficiency on the part of those responsible.[90] Of the four men carrying out the valuation, two were York stationers. Francis Mawburne was, like Mark Foster, associated with the printer Stephen Bulkley. Ralph Brocklebank, another of the valuers, had his premises 'in the Minster Yard'.[91] For whatever reason, the stationer's shop was doing far less business than in John Foster's time.

Table 13.   Foster's inventory compared with inventories from other provincial towns

	York 1616	Hereford 1695	Penrith 1698
	copies	titles	copies
Bibles, prayer-books & catechisms	407 (12.1%)	0	60 (5.1%)
Religion, sermons	564 (16.7%)	70 (42.7%)	160 (13.7%)
School-books	938 (27.8%)	31 (18.9%)	675 (57.6%)
Instruction/law	142 (4.2%)	17 (10.4%)	97 (8.3%)
Verse	42 (1.3%)	0	11 (0.9%)
History/politics	75 (2.2%)	12 (7.3%)	18 (1.5%)
Travel/geography	8 (0.2%)	3 (1.8%)	3 (0.3%)
Literature	69 (2.1%)	8 (4.9%)	0
Science/medicine	44 (1.3%)	1 (0.6%)	0
Miscellaneous*	685 (20.3%)	22 (13.4%)	30 (2.6%)
Not known	399 (11.8%)	0	117 (10.0%)
Total volumes	3373	164	1171

* conflates Isaac's categories of sociology and biography; includes for Foster 604 almanacs.

If one looks beyond York, to other provincial towns for which booksellers' inventories survive for the seventeenth century, the question of comparison is no more satisfactory. We know of thirteen inventories from the period 1600–1700 for provincial English towns (excluding Oxford, Cambridge, and Scottish booksellers as different in kind). These are as follows: 1603 Norwich, 1612 Manchester, 1615 Exeter, 1616 York

---

[90] Welford, op. cit. (note 46); P. Wenham. *The Great and Close Siege of York* (Kineton, 1970), pp. 14–16.
[91] In 1666 Mawburne and Bulkley were arrested for printing and selling seditious papers, and a letter written to Secretary Williamson on Mawburne's behalf describes him as 'quiet but weak in business' (Plomer, op. cit. (note 2)).

(John Foster), 1617 Lincoln, 1629 Norwich, 1644 York (Mark Foster), 1644 Hull, 1648 Warrington, 1677 Warwick, 1679 Coventry, 1695 Hereford, and 1698 Penrith. Not all of these are in print, and not all give sufficient detail to allow comparisons of stock.[92] Nearest to John Foster's in size, but much later in the century, is the inventory of John Benson of Penrith (1698) with 1,171 copies valued at £74 17s. 3½d. In his analysis of the Penrith inventory, Peter Isaac gives a breakdown of the stock by subject both for Benson's 1698 stock and for the stock of Williams in Hereford (1695).[93] It is possible, therefore, to compare these two inventories with the Foster 1616 stock by subject category (Table 13).

The differences between the inventories of Foster in York and Benson in Penrith are clear: the Penrith bookseller had a much higher proportion of school and educational texts, which formed the basis of his trade, and apart from religious books and books of instruction there are no other sizeable categories of stock. Foster, on the other hand, had a wider variety of kinds of book in stock, and school-books and religious books did not dominate. Comparison with the Hereford stock is more problematic: as well as the disparity in time (which applies also, of course, to the comparison with the Penrith stock) there is a greater disparity in the size of the business. The Hereford bookseller's stock is very small by comparison with the other two; moreover, the stock has been measured in titles rather than volumes, which may well distort the comparison. None the less, the Foster list is less heavily weighted towards religious books. Interestingly, the Hereford bookseller has a high proportion of books which are neither religious nor educational texts, and is therefore more like Foster in this respect than is Benson of Penrith. Since the basis for such detailed comparison is too flimsy for any firm conclusions, it is worth attempting to give an impression of Foster's business in the context provided by other inventories of the provincial trade which allow subject analysis. Table 14 opposite uses the three broad categories of book used earlier in the subject analysis of Foster's books to offer a comparison of Foster's stock with those of five other seventeenth-century provincial

[92] Apart from the inventories of John and Mark Foster, these are: Gilbert (1603 Norwich), D. Stoker, 'The Norwich book trade before 1800', *Transactions of the Cambridge Bibliographical Society*, 8 (1981), 79–125; Browne (1612 Manchester), J. P. Earwaker, 'Notes on the early booksellers and stationers of Manchester prior to the year 1700', *Transactions of the Lancashire and Cheshire Antiquarian Society*, 6 (1889), 2–26; James (1629 Norwich), D. Stoker op. cit. (note 92); Awdley (1644 Hull), C. W. Chilton, 'The inventory of a provincial bookseller's stock of 1644', *The Library*, 6th series, 1 (1979), 126–43; Booth (1647/48 Warrington), W. H. Rylands, 'Booksellers and stationers in Warrington, 1639 to 1657, with the full list of the contents of a stationer's shop there in 1647', *Transactions of the Historic Society of Lancashire and Cheshire*, 37 (=n.s. 1) for 1885 (1888), 67–115; Mountford (1677 Warwick), P. Morgan, 'The Warwick bookseller: Richard Mountford, 1677', in N. Alcock (ed.), *The Past in Warwick: Tudors to Victorians* (Coventry, 1955), pp. 31–35; Brooke (1679 Coventry), summary given in P. Morgan, op. cit. (note 86); Williams (1695 Hereford), F. C. Morgan, 'A Hereford bookseller's catalogue of 1696', *Transactions of the Woolhope Naturalists' Field Club*, 31 (1942), 22–36; Benson (1698 Penrith), P. Isaac, *History of the Book Trade in the North: an inventory of books sold by a seventeenth-century Penrith grocer* (Wylam, 1989). Ian Maxted kindly sent details of the 1615 inventory of the Exeter bookseller, Michael Hart, but too late to include here. Hart's stock totalled some 4,500 books worth just over £100 (information from Ian Maxted). Hart's business, then, was very similar in scale to Foster's, and a comparison of the two would be a valuable extension of the present work.
[93] Isaac, op. cit. (note 92), p. 7.

Table 14. Comparison of Foster's stock with those of other provincial booksellers

	York 1616	Hull 1644	Warrington 1648	Warwick 1677	Hereford 1695	Penrith 1698
Religion	28.8%	36.9%	31.9%	18.9%	42.7%	18.8%
School-books	27.8%	43.7%	57.7%	81.1%	18.9%	57.6%
All others	31.6%	13.9%	2.5%	—	38.4%	13.6%
Not known	11.8%	5.6%	7.9%	—	—	10.0%

booksellers. Most of these booksellers, it would seem, were catering very specifically for local clergy and schoolmasters: in Hull, Warrington, Warwick, and Penrith more than 75% of the stock consisted of religious and educational books, and indeed in Warwick these constituted the entire stock. Only the Hereford shop, also in a cathedral city, is comparable with Foster's in its proportion of 'other' subject categories, though the counting of titles rather than volumes and the relatively small size of the stock may be distorting factors; Hereford has, too, a particularly high proportion of religious books, which distinguishes it from Foster's. In general, then, Foster's is a stock more evenly balanced between the three categories than that of the other provincial booksellers whose detailed inventories have been worked on.

Conclusion

In conclusion, John Foster's inventory has proved both a rich source for book-trade history in its own right and the starting point for a study of the York book trade and its customers in the early seventeenth century. It has been possible to set the detailed analysis of the inventory itself in a three-dimensional context: by investigating the material circumstances of bookselling and bookbinding in the Minster Yard; by examining family and trade relationships among York book-trade personnel; and by using the list of debtors to gain an insight into the market for books amongst both religious and lay readers in York and its surrounding area. At the same time, this study further illustrates the need, identified by Paul Morgan, for further work on provincial booksellers in other towns and cities in order to provide a firmer comparative base.

APPENDIX 1

Corrections and Additions to Robert Davies's Transcript of John Foster's Inventory (York, 1616)

Robert Davies's transcript of the inventory of the York bookseller, John Foster, was printed in Appendix B to his *A Memoir of the York Press* (1868).* His work is an accurate and careful account of the large majority of Foster's printed books and equipment. However, apart from the occasional omission of an entry and infrequent errors, he decided to simplify the entries for bibles, psalms, and psalters, and also mostly to omit the records of paper or parchment books, and of single old books. He also failed to transcribe the list of Foster's debtors. The following list corrects and expands Davies's transcript.

Foster's inventory is Probate Inventory L1/17(38) in York Minster Library. It is a parchment roll, made up of 17 membranes sewn together. The roll is 5¾ inches wide, and the first membrane is approximately 30 inches long. It is well preserved and is clearly written. The roll begins with inventory of Foster's goods and chattels made on 25 November 1616 (Davies, pp. 372–74). This is followed by the inventory of his books and equipment made the following day (Davies, pp. 342–71). The roll concludes with a list of Foster's leases and debtors, as Davies reports.

Davies's transcription silently expands contractions and usually gives the exact spelling, normalizing 'u' to 'v'. The list which follows is keyed to Davies's printed transcript by Davies page number and by item number counting from top to bottom, distinguishing, where appropriate, left-hand columns by 'l' and right-hand columns by 'r' and identifying additional items by 'a', 'b', 'c', etc.

Inventory of the goods and chattels (25 November 1616)

372.l.15: for 'one other covered chaire' read 'one other little covered chaire'.

373.l.17: the 'three course towells' were appraised at 'xii^d' (not 'ii^d').

374.l.08: the 'little drippinge pann . . .' was appraised at 'xvi^d' (not 'xvi^s').

Inventory of books in the shop (26 November 1616)

342.02: contracted from:

a	It one [Bible] lesser print	xxxviii^s
b	It one Bible in small folio roman	
	wth Com bost & buft	xvii^s vi^d

* *A Memoir of the York Press with Notices of Authors, Printers, and Stationers in the Sixteenth, Seventeenth, and Eighteenth Centuries* (London, 1868; rptd. York, 1988, with introduction by Bernard Barr), pp. 342–74.

c   It one other in folio plaine roman
     wth Com   xv^s
d   It one in folio engl[ish] wth psalmes
     plain Claspes   xv^s
e   It one Com & psalmes in folio   vi^s viii^d

344.r.08: Davies contracts the inventory's list of Cooke's 7th–11th parts:

a   It one Cookes seventh p^t   iii^s iii^d
b   It one Cookes eight p^t   xx^s
c   It one Cookes ninth p^t   viii^s
d   It one Cookes tenth p^t   viii^s vi^d
e   It one Cookes eleaventh p^t   iiii^s vi^d

344.r.10: after item 10 add entries:

a   It one parchment book   iiii^s
b   It one paper book in folio 8 q^rs Claspes   iii^s iiii^d

344.r.12: after item 12 add entry:

a   It one Cornu Copia   v^s

344.r.13: after item 13 add entry:

a   It one old postell in lattin   xxiii^d

345.l.02: Davies contracts and omits valuation:

a   It two [bibles] plaine wth ouills   xxvi^s
b   It one bible old roman bb   x^s vi^d
c   It three new engl[ish] bost and buft   xxxxvii^s vi^d
d   It one bible new wth Concorda engl[ish]   xii^s vi^d
e   It one in phillits wth Concorda engl[ish]   xii^s vi^d

345.r.15: item 15 follows 345.r.06 in inventory.

345.r.12: Davies contracts and omits valuation:

a   Item one Com Testament & psalmes in 4to   vii^d
b   It one Com & psalmes great letter   iiii^s iiii^d
c   It one Com & psalmes in 4to phill   iiii^s
d   It two Com & psalmes plaine   vii^s iii^d
e   It one Testament & psalmes plaine   ii^s
f   It one single psalter   xxii^d

348.r.04: after item 04 add entry:

a   It one disputatio bible   xvi^d

349.r.07: item 07 follows 349.l.11 in inventory.

349.r.10: after item 10 add entry:

a   It one booke of posteles in engl[ish]   xii^d

349.r.13: after item 13 add entry:

a	It two paper bookes in lether	iiii^{s} viii^{d}

350.1.02: Davies contracts and omits valuation:

a	Item one bible in 8to gilt edge	vii^{s} vi^{d}
b	It one bible in 8to phill Claspes	vii^{s}
c	It one bible in 8to bb wth services	vii^{s} ii^{d}
d	It one old bible bb	iiii^{s}
e	It one Com test & psalmes All gilt	v^{s} iiii^{d}
f	It one Com test & psal ph	iiii^{s}
g	It one Com booke gilt edge & corners	iiii^{s}
h	It one Com in 8to phill & claspes	iii^{s}
i	It foure Com test & psalmes plaine	xiii^{s} viii^{d}
j	It foure psalters test & psalmes	xiii^{s} iiii^{d}
k	It ten single test in 8to	xiii^{s} iiii^{d}
l	It nyne Com bookes in 8to	xxiiii^{s}
m	It two paper bookes in 8to one ph: one gilt	iii^{s} ii^{d}

351.1.11: inventory adds 'in 8to ph Cla:'.

351.1.15, 355.r.01: these two entries are entered together with an overall value of 'x^{d}'.

351.r.07–09: entered together with an overall value of 'viii^{s}'; Davies mistakenly enters each individually at that price.

353.1.08: 'Apthonius' valued at 'iii^{s}'.

353.r.11: the two 'Justius' books are valued at 'xiiii^{d}' not 'xiii^{d}'.

353.r.16 and 17 are transposed.

354.1.03: after item 03 add entry:

a	It one single psalter	ix^{d}

355.1. 07 and 08: given in a single entry valued together at 'vi^{d}'.

355.r.17: for 'Qualpercus' read 'Qualbergius'.

356.r.16: for 'Indies' read 'Indians'.

357.1. 06 and 07: a combined entry priced at 'xii^{d}' (i.e. 6d. each?).

357.1.14: after item 14 add entry:

a	It one Com & psalmes phil Claspes	ii^{s} iiii^{d}

357.1.15: inventory notes that these are 'ph[illets]'.

357.1.16: after item 16 add entry:

a	It one Imitation whole ph	xx^{d}

357.1.17 ('One Pensive . . .'): should be included as part of block entry in right-hand column (i.e., not valued at 'v^s vi^d').

359.1.02 and r.01: a single entry as follows:

a   Item one Conduitt of Comfort in ph ⎫
b   It one pretius pearle in fillits   ⎬   ii^s vi^d
    Davies gives a figure of 'x^d' for each (instead of 'xv^d'?).

359.r.03: after item 3 add entry:

a   It one third part of the bible   viii^d

359.r.06: The section headed 'Bookes in 16, plaine' is given as a block entry valued at 'iii^s'. There are five additional entries immediately following item 359.r.06:

a   It eight Com & psalmes in 16   xiiii^s viii^d
b   It three single Testaments in 16   ii^s iii^d
c   It five singinge of psalmes in 16   iii^s iiii^d
d   It two seruis & psalmes in small print   xii^d
e   It one godly garden wth psalms old   iiii^d

359.1.10: Valerius Maximus valued at 'ii^s iiii^d' not 'ii^s iii^d'.

359.1.19: after item 19 add entry:

a   It one lattin Testament   vi^d

359.r.09: omit 'Lattin'.

360.r.08: after item 08 add entry:

a   It two parts of the bible in lattin   viii^d

360.r.11: Davies combines two entries preceding item 10:

a   It three gilt primers   xii^d
b   It one plaine primer   iii^d

360.1.12: entry contracted from eight entries:

a   Item one Com Testa & psalmes gilt   iii^s ii^d
b   It one Com testa & psalmes Cross gilt   iii^s viii^d
c   It one Testa & psalmes cross gilt   iii^s
d   It one testa & psalmes cross gilt edge   ii^s vii^d
e   It one Com & psalmes gilt   ii^s vi^d
f   It one testa & psalmes cross ph   ii^s iii^d
g   It one testa & psalmes Clasped   xxii^d
h   It one psalter & psalmes fillits   xiiii^d

360.1.13, 360.r.13: both entries inaccurately contracted from:

a   Item two psalmes engl[ish] ph Claspes   xxii^d
b   It two psalms gilt engl[ish] letter   ii^s vi^d
c   It three gilt edge engl[ish] letter   iii^s vi^d

d	It two psalters & psalmes gilt edge	iii^s
e	It three psalmes roman Claspes	ii^s vi^d
f	It two gilt edge roman	ii^s ii^d
g	It one dull gilt roman	xiiii^d
h	It nynetene prayers in 32 silvered	ii^s iiii^d
i	It twelve bibles cross silvered	iii^s
j	It one psalter & one psalmes old	vi^d

360.14: (title above should read: 'Writeinge Tables of sortes in 16') contracted from:

a	Item three paire dull gilt best sorte	iii^s vi^d
b	It seaven paire of little tables gilt	ii^s iiii^d
c	It twenty three paire of large white Tables	v^s viii^d
d	It thirty one paire of number thre	v^s
e	It twenty of the least sorte	ii^s viii^d

360.r.21: ('Twenty-two paper bookes . . .') contracted from:
paper bookes in folio

a	Item one paper booke of Ryall paper of five queares in forrell	vii^s vi^d
b	It one of Duch paper two queares	ii^s
c	It one other of Duch paper of two queares & twelve sheetes in vellam	ii^s
d	It one of three quears pott paper in forrell	xiiii^d
e	It one of Ruled paper two queares	xx^d
f	It three of two queares A peece in narrow folio	ii^s
g	It foure in quarto of two queares A peece	ii^s viii^d
h	It two in quarto of one queare A peece	viii^d
i	It seaven paper bookes in quarto wth notes written in them	iii^s vi^d
j	It one paper booke in folio two queares	viii^d

361.l.06 and r.02 are transposed.

361.l.11: after item 11 add entry:

a	It one Country Contentment	xv^d

362.l.05 and 06 are transposed.

362.l.08 and 09 are transposed.

362.r.02: value should be 'xiiii^d' (not 'xviii^d').

362.r.10: after item 10 add entry:

a   It two small Coppy bookes   viii^d

363.r.02: contracted from:

a   It eighteene bookes in quarto   iiii^s
b   It threscore sticht bookes litle works ⎤
c   It forty four sticht bookes litle works ⎦   iiii^s

363.l.09: ('Seaven'): value should be 'ii^s xi^d' (not 'ii^s vi^d').

363.r.11–13: the catechisms gathered together as item 14 occur between these three
    entries:

a   It eleaven perkins Cattachismes   xviii^d
b   It ten more Cattachismes   xiiii^d
c   It eight Egertons Catta   xvi^d
d   It nine padgets Catta   xii^d
e   It three nowells Catta   xii^d
     [Item 12]
f   It one Dentes Cattachismes   ii^d

364.l.18: for 'Nides' read 'Nids'.

364.r.05: value should be 'v^d' (not 'iii^d').

365.r.14 and 15: these two items bracketed together with a single price, 'xviii^d', for all
    seven books.

366.r.16: condensed from:

a   It two servis & one psalms in large quarto   xviii^d
b   It two psalmes for Com in quarto q^{res} iii^s viii^d
c   It foure psalmes for bibles in octavo queares   ii^s iiii^d
d   It six of psalmes in octavo queares   v^s vi^d

367.l.04: after item 04 add entry:

a   It one Com & psalms in octavo queares   ii^s

367.l.18: after item 18 add entry:
a   It two paper bookes   vi^d

367.r.03: after item 03 add entries:

a   It one psalter and psalmes queares   xx^d
b   It two psalmes in four parts   iii^s iiii^d

367.r.21 and 22: these are a single entry at a lower joint price, thus:

         It two Seatons Logicke & one Justin   ii^s

367.r.25, 368.l.01: recorded as a joint entry worth 'x^d'; Davies splits the sum between the two entries, but there is 1 'Sin against the Holy Ghost' and 2 'Christian Armoury'.

368.l.04: after item 04 add entry:

a   It one of psalmes in octavo queares   xi^d

368.r.01: after item 01 add entries:

a   It one bible & psalmes in octavo   vi^d
b   It one psalter in octavo   vii^d

368.r.04: after item 04 add entry:

a   It one Aesopp fables   viii^d

368.r.10 and 11 are transposed.

368.r.16: value should be 'xvi^d' (not 'xiii^d').

369.l.01: after item 01 add entry:

a   It two of psalmes   xxi^d

369.r.07: ('Jeroms Bible'): in inventory this occurs after 369.l.05.

369.l.10: after item 10 add entry:

a   It one old lattin dictionary   ii^s vi^d

370.l.07: after item 07 add entry, to be included in group price:

a   It foure old lattin gramers

370.l.13: after item 13 add entry:

a   It one old gramer   iii^d

370.l.18 occurs after 370.l.19 in inventory.

370.l.19: after item 19 add entries:

a   It ten other in octavo   xx^d
b   It five old bookes in sixteene   vi^d

370.l.20: part of a double entry, one of which is omitted, followed by an additional entry:

a   It one old gramer Construed   }
b   It one nowells Catta greek & lattin   }   vi^d
c   It ten old stiched bookes in octavo   iiii^d

370.l.21: after item 21 add entry:

a   It one other little booke in lattin   iii^d

371.r.04: after item 04 add entry:

a   It shelves in the kitchinge
b   It shelves in the wairehouse ⎫
c   It one forme of wainscott   ⎭   v^s

371.r.05: after item 05 add entry:

a   Item one Baskett of Bookes
     with some of them perfect and
     other unperfect with
     waste paper   viii^s

Summa bon*orum*

Item one Lease of one Close att the
bardike [i.e., Bur Dyke] not worth the yearly rent

Item one Lease of/one/Stable parte
of y^t in m^r Francis wodd yard &
the other parte in Willm
Blanchard yard & the stable
baye with Geistes in the Chamber   xl^s

Item one Lease of one Close
neare unto the freeschoole in
Gelegate [i.e., Gillygate] not worth the yearly Rent

Item debts oweing unto the deceased

Item Mr Dunwell of Wetherby
the seaventh of February 1615   iiii^s ix^d

Item Edward Secker the
twenty seaventh of July 1611   xiii^s vi^d

Item George Townson the
twenty one of September 1616   xxv^s x^d

Item Mr Wilson Attorney the
twenty seaventh of January 1613   iiii^s

Item Mr Claphamson the
fourteenth of maye 1616   xxiiii^s vi^d

Item Mr Staveley the
fifth of march 1612   vi^d

Item Mr Slator the
twelveth of July 1613   xviii^d

Item Mr Millington his Cussen
the eightht of october 1614   xii^d

Item Mr Squier the
nyneteenth of July 1616   xxxiiii^s x^d

Item Mr Leake the twenty
fifth of september 1616   xxiiii^s ii^d

Item Mr Jagure the
eighteenth of May 1616   xliii^s x^d

Item Mr Fairebanke of thirlebery
the twenty seaventh of october 1614   v^s vi^d

Item Mr Williamson sadler
the twenty three of January 1615   xv^d

It Thomas Williamson
the nynth of February 1614   ii^s vii^d

Item Mr Walter the
twenty fourth of october   xiiii^s

Item Mr Bubwith of Rothwell
the third of october 1616   xiii^s vi^d

Item Mr Cooke my Lord
presidents Chaplin the
twenty sixth of September 1616   viii^s

Item Mr Smyth my Lord
Presidents Chaplin the
eight of February 1614   v^s iiii^d

Item Mr Greenewood the
twenty fourth of January 1615   xxv^s iii^d

Item Daniell Bell the
Eleaventh of october 1615   xxi^s

Item Mr Standeuen the
nynteenth of August 1612   ii^s

Item Mr Greene of heslington
the nynteenth of may 1612   viii^d

Item Mr Bankes of horton
the fifth of october 1615   vii^s vi^d

Item Sr Edward Stanapp
the nyth of July 1616   iiii^d

Item Mr Willm Best
the nynth of maye 1614   ii^s vi^d

Item Mr Sandwith the
seaventeenthe of August 1616   v^s ii^d

Item Robert Walmsley   x^s viii^d

It Doctor Bankes the
third of June 1614   viii^s

Item Mr Sadler the sixt of June 1616   iiii^s vii^d

Item Mr Cockson the eight of August 1615   ii^s ii^d

Item Mt John watt of Thearne
the twenty two of Aprill 1616   iiii^s

Item Mr Smythson draper
the sixt of november 1611   iii^s iiii^d

Item Mr Walker of stillingflete
the eight of october 1611   iiii^s

Item Mr Smyth of Caruerley
upon bond the nynth of Aprill 1615   xx^s

Item Mr Hickson the
nyneteenth of october 1616   xii^d

Item Mr Wade the sixteenth of Febru 1614   iii^d

It. Mr Leng of strensall the
eighteenth of December 1612   vi^d

Item Mr Dodsworth the twenty
five of June 1612   iiii^s viii^d

Item George Dickinson the
tenth of August 1613   iii^s xi^d

It Tomisin Watterworth the
eighteenth of Aprill 1613   iii^s

Item Mr Sanderson the
fifteenth of Aprill 1613   xii^d

Item Tristram Britton the
sixteenth of July 1612   vi^d

Item Mr Belwodd the xvth of may 1616   xxvi^s

APPENDIX 2

Identification of Works in the Inventory of John Foster's Books

This appendix lists in alphabetical order by author all the books in Foster's inventory, merging the additional and corrected items from Appendix 1 with the items printed by Davies. Non-book items listed in the inventory of the bookshop are also included, some of them grouped under appropriate headings (e.g. paper, paper books), and others at the end of the list. The purpose of this appendix is to provide the reader with a short-title, quick-reference list of the books contained in the inventory. It is not, however, intended as a fully annotated edition of the inventory. The reader interested in how many copies Foster had in stock, in details of format and binding, or in the value of individual works, is directed to Davies and to Appendix I by a system of index numbers described below.

Column 1

The first column gives, as precisely as possible, appropriate reference numbers from the catalogues used. These are usually *STC* numbers, or (when prefaced by 'Ad') numbers from H. M. Adams, *Catalogue of Books Printed on the Continent of Europe, 1501–1600 in Cambridge Libraries*, 2 vols. (Cambridge, 1967). If identifications of both title and edition can be made with precision and reasonable certainty, the numbers stand alone. Question marks preceding numbers indicate a degree of tentativeness in the identification. Where considerable uncertainty prevails, the abbreviation 'cf.' is placed before numbers and spans of numbers. Such spans, when prefaced by 'cf.', may include editions in formats other than the one specified in the inventory. Occasionally the whole span identified is in the 'wrong' format, in which case Foster's is likely to be a lost edition.

The possibility that an otherwise unidentified item is a continental book is signalled by the abbreviation 'cont.', which is followed where appropriate by the letters BL (=British Library), BN (=Bibliothèque Nationale), or NUC (=National Union Catalog) if the book has been found in any of those catalogues. In cases where nothing corresponding to the inventory item has been found in *STC*, Adams, or any of the library catalogues consulted, the following conventions are used: '0' indicates an unidentified item, or one where identification by edition is impossible (as in the case of bibles); the word 'lost' indicates that an inventory title has not been otherwise identified and may have been entirely lost from the record; 'n' indicates a non-book item, where a reference number would be irrelevant.

Columns 2 and 3

Except in a few cases where certainty is impossible, authors' names are regularized in modern form. Titles which can be securely identified are given as they appear in *STC*,

Adams, or another modern work of reference. Where, on the other hand, precise identification of a title is impossible, the title is transcribed from Davies or from Appendix 1 in inverted commas within square brackets. Square brackets with no inverted commas are as they appear in *STC*.

Column 4

The fourth column provides an index number to enable identification of individual items as printed by Davies or in our Appendix 1. Entries in Davies's transcription of the inventory (printed as his Appendix B) are listed by page number, column (left or right), and entry number counting from the top of the page. Thus the item numbered '359.r.19' will be found as the nineteenth item in the right-hand column of Davies's page 359. Items which are additions to Davies's version of the inventory or which have been corrected in any way, and which appear in sequence in our Appendix 1, are flagged with an asterisk. They are keyed to Davies by the system just described but are only to be found in Appendix 1 above. Lower-case letters (a, b, c, d . . .) are used here and in Appendix 1 to indicate the order of such additional items.

STC, Adams, or other reference	Author	Title	Davies no.
?698a	A-Parisiis, Francis	Consilia medicinalia	344.1.16
cf. 17.7–20.8	A.B.C.	['Foure-score A B Ces']	364.r.07
cf. 17.7–20.8	A.B.C.	['One hundred A B Ces']	368.1.05
cf. 17.7–20.8	A.B.C.	['Twelve Abces']	370.1.18
cf. 21.4–21.5/lost	Hornbooks	['Eight Horne Bookes']	364.r.09
48–50.5	Abbot, Robert	A defence of the Reformed catholicke	346.r.09
?187	Aesop	['One Esopp Fables, with a comment']	356.1.03
cf. 168–89	Aesop	['one Aesopp fables']	368.r.04a*
cf. 168–89	Aesop	['Eight Aesopp Fables']	353.r.14
cf. 168–89	Aesop	['Seaven Aesopp Fables']	367.r.02
cf. 168–89	Aesop	['Two Aesopp Fables']	353.r.10
?179–82	Aesop	The fables of Esope in Englysshe with all his lyfe	367.r.19
?189.5	Affectation	Of affectation a morall discourse	351.1.08
?Ad A355–66	Agricola, Rudolphus	['One Olde Rudolphius Greek gramer']	349.r.11
cf. Ad A374–94	Agrippa, Henricus Cornelius	['One Cornelius Agrippa']	370.1.09
cf. Ad A601–12	Alciatus, Andreas	Emblematum liber	354.1.04
356	Alison, Richard (professor of music)	Cantus primus . . . An howres recreation in musicke	361.1.05
364	Allen, Robert	The doctrine of the gospel	343.r.03
376.7	Alliston, Joseph	The christians guide	358.1.02
?376.7	Alliston, Joseph	['Two Allestons Meditations']	357.1.20
cf. 389–403.9	Almanacks	['Fifty-four Alminackes']	364.r.08
cf. 389–403.9	Almanacks	['Five hundred and fifty Alminackes of sortes']	368.r.02
435.39–35.59	Almanacks: Digges, Leonard	A prognostication euerlasting	362.1.07
439.3–39.23	Almanacks: Erra Pater	The pronostycacyon for euer	364.1.01
0	?Ames, William	['One Stiltetus Medulla Patrum']	348.r.10
?cont.	Anania, Giovanni Lorenzo	['One Fabrica dell Mondo in French']	344.r.01
cf. 596–629	Andrewes, Lancelot (bishop)	['Three Bishoppe of Elies Sermons']	366.1.03
604	Andrewes, Lancelot (bishop)	Responsio ad apologiam cardinalis Bellarmini	349.r.03

STC, Adams, or other reference	Author	Title	Davies no.
626–26.5	Andrewes, Lancelot (bishop)	Tortura Torti: sive, ad Matthaei Torti librum responsio	365.r.11
645–50	Anglerius, Petrus Martyr	The decades of the newe worlde or west India	346.r.07
?645–50	Anglerius, Petrus Martyr	The decades of the newe worlde or west India	356.r.16*
cont./NUC	Anon.	Pieces dv memorable proces	356.l.09
1599–99.7	Anon.	A beautifull baybush	359.l.01
14416–18	Anon.	Deus & Rex: sive dialogus	364.r.05*
14419–20.7	Anon.	God and the king: or, a dialogue	363.l.07
21299–99.7	Anon.	[Seven wise masters of Rome.]	364.l.10
cf. 700–04	Aphthonius	Aphthonii sophistae Progymnasmata	353.l.08*
cf. 700–04	Aphthonius	Aphthonii sophistae Progymnasmata	356.r.11
cf. 700–04	Aphthonius	Aphthonii sophistae Progymnasmata	357.r.07
cf. 700–04	Aphthonius	Aphthonii sophistae Progymnasmata	367.l.16
cf. 700–04	Aphthonius	Aphthonii sophistae Progymnasmata	370.l.13
cf. Ad A1340–61	Appian	['One Appianii']	360.l.01
?758/cont.	Aristotle	['One Aristotles Phisickes']	356.l.08
?758/cont.	Aristotle	['One Aristotles Phisickes']	359.r.12
?753–53.5	Aristotle	['One Aristotles Ethickes']	356.r.14
?20157/Ad A1863–71	Aristotle	['One Aristotle Orgonon']	354.r.13
?20157/cont.	Aristotle	['One Aristotles Logick']	357.l.11
?Ad A1734–35	Aristotle	['One Aristotle in Greeke']	369.l.14
?761	Aristotle	['One Aristotles Problems']	359.r.11
?762–65.3	Aristotle	The problemes of Aristotle	364.r.04
Ad A1910–12	Aristotle	['One Aristotles Politickes in Greeke']	345.r.02
cf. Ad A1940–53	Aristotle	['Two Aristotle Retorick']	356.l.16
?cont.	Aristotle	['One Aristotles Topicorum']	356.l.02
Ad A1849	Aristotle	Commentariorum P. Fonsecae . . . tomus primus/secundus	345.l.11
cf. 826–29	Ascham, Roger	Dissertissimi viri Rogeri Aschami . . . familiarium epistolarum libri tres	359.r.15

STC, Adams, or other reference	Author	Title	Davies no.
826–29	Ascham, Roger	Dissertissimi viri Rogeri Aschami . . . familiarium epistolarum libri tres	368.1.10
832–36	Ascham, Roger	The scholemaster	370.r.01
890	Attersoll, William	A commentarie upon . . . Paul to Philemon	343.1.09
890	Attersoll, William	A commentarie upon . . . Paul to Philemon	365.1.01
898	Attersoll, William	The pathway to Canaan	347.1.10
889.5	Attersoll, William	The new covenant	365.1.09
0	Augustine	['One Augustines Sermons']	344.r.15
953.5	Augustine	The sinners glasse	358.1.01
988	Avity, Pierre d'	The estates, empires, & principallities	343.1.01
1012–13	Ayrault, Pierre	A discourse for parents honour	363.r.07
1088	Babington, Gervase	Comfortable notes . . . Leviticus	348.1.14
1077	Babington, Gervase	The workes of the right reverend G. Babington	343.1.10
1209.5–16	Baker, Humphrey	The well sprynge of sciences	354.r.15
1219–22	Baker, John	Lectures . . . upon the xii. articles of our christian faith	351.1.01
1253–66	Baldwin, William	A treatise of morall phylosophie	354.r.12
1387–88	Barclay, John	Joannis Barclaii poematum libri duo	345.r.01
14466–66.5	Bathe, William	Janua linguarum, sive modus maxime accommodatus	346.r.11
1601.5–02.7	Bayly, Lewis	The practise of pietie	357.1.13
1601.5–02.7	Bayly, Lewis	The practise of pietie	368.1.07
1724.5–29.5	Becon, Thomas	The gouernans of vertue	357.1.23
1724.5–29.5	Becon, Thomas	The gouernans of vertue	358.1.03
1756.5–71	Becon, Thomas	The sycke mannes salue	350.r.14
1777	Beda	Axiomata philosophica	355.1.06
1782–82.5	Bédé, Jean	The right, and prerogative of kings	350.r.09
1782	Bédé, Jean	The right, and prerogative of kings	367.r.11
1782	Bédé, Jean	The right, and prerogative of kings	368.1.03
1823	Bell, Thomas	The hunting of the romish foxe	363.r.10
1824	Bell, Thomas	The jesuites antepast	348.r.08
?cont.	Bellarmine, Robert	['Two Bellarmines Epetomij']	345.1.07

5

STC, Adams, or other reference	Author	Title	Davies no.
1895–96	Benvenuto	Il passagiere	348.r.05
1952.5–53	Bernard, Richard	Josuahs godly resolution	363.r.13
1958	Bernard, Richard	Plaine evidences	347.r.08
1963.7	Bernard, Richard	A staffe of comfort	358.1.14
1963.7	Bernard, Richard	A staffe of comfort	368.r.10
0	?Bernard	['One Bernerd Decretalis']	369.1.08
Ad B823	Bertramus, Bonaventura Cornelius	Comparatio grammaticae Hebraicae	345.1.15
2006–06.5	Bèze, Théodore de	Confessio christianae fidei	355.1.04
2019–20	Bèze, Théodore de	Job expounded	352.1.09
0	Bible	['eight Com & psalmes in 16']	359.r.06a*
0	Bible	['Eight Psalters in sixteene']	368.r.14
0	Bible	['five singinge of psalmes in 16']	359.r.06c*
0	Bible	['foure Com test & psalmes plaine']	350.1.02i*
0	Bible	['foure psalmes for bibles in octavo queares']	366.r.16c*
0	Bible	['foure psalters test & psalmes']	350.1.02j*
0	Bible	['Four Psalmes in thirty-two']	369.r.01
cf. 2802–2810	Bible	Jesu Christi d.n. nouum testamentum, T. Beza interprete	356.r.19
0	Bible	['nyne Com bookes in 8to']	350.1.02l*
0	Bible	['One Apocraph of the Bible with Psalmes']	364.r.02
0	Bible	['One Beazaes Testament, Greek and Lattin']	354.1.06
0	Bible	['one bible & psalmes in octavo']	368.r.01a*
0	Bible	['one bible in folio of the largest sorte']	342.01
0	Bible	['One Bible in 4to. Roman new b.b.']	345.1.01
0	Bible	['one bible in 8to bb wth services']	350.1.02c*
0	Bible	['one bible in 8to gilt edge']	350.1.02a*
0	Bible	['one bible in 8to phill Claspes']	350.1.02b*
0	Bible	['one Bible in small folio roman W^th Com bost & buft']	342.02b*
0	Bible	['one [Bible] lesser print']	342.02a*

STC, Adams, or other reference	Author	Title	Davies no.
0	Bible	['one bible new wth Concorda engl[ish]']	345.1.02d*
0	Bible	['one bible old roman bb']	345.1.02b*
0	Bible	['One Bible Servis and one Genologie']	365.r.13
0	Bible	['one booke of posteles in engl[ish]']	349.r.10a*
0	Bible	['one Com & psalmes gilt']	360.1.12e*
0	Bible	['one Com & psalmes great letter']	345.r.12b*
0	Bible	['one Com & psalmes in folio']	342.02e*
0	Bible	['one Com & psalmes in 4to phill']	345.r.12c*
0	Bible	['one Com & psalmes phil Claspes']	357.1.14a*
0	Bible	['one Com & psalms in octavo queares']	367.1.04a*
0	Bible	['one Com booke gilt edge & corners']	350.1.02g*
0	Bible	['one Com in 8to phill & claspes']	350.1.02h*
0	Bible	['One Comon Testament and Psalmes']	345.r.11
0	Bible	['one Com testa & psalmes Cross gilt']	360.1.12b*
0	Bible	['one Com Testa & psalmes gilt']	360.1.12a*
0	Bible	['one Com Testament & psalmes in 4to']	345.r.12a*
0	Bible	['one Com test & psalmes All gilt']	350.1.02e*
0	Bible	['one Com test & psal ph']	350.1.02f*
0	Bible	['One Concordantia Magna']	345.1.03
0	Bible	['one dull gilt roman']	360.1.13g*
0	?Bible	['One Flores Bibliae']	359.r.13
0	Bible	['one in folio engl[ish] wth psalmes plain Claspes']	342.02d*
0	Bible	['one in phillits wth Concorda engl[ish]']	345.1.02e*
0	Bible	['One Jeroms Bible']	369.r.07
0	Bible	['one lattin Testament']	359.1.19a*
0	Bible	['One Middleborough Psalmes, gilt']	358.1.20

STC, Adams, or other reference	Author	Title	Davies no.
0	Bible	['One Midleborough Psalmes']	368.r.11
?cont	Bible	['One Musterius Hebrew and Lattin Bible']	369.l.09
0	Bible	['one of psalmes in octavo queares']	368.l.04a*
0	Bible	['one old bible bb']	350.l.02d*
0	Bible	['One Olde booke of Moses']	355.r.08
0	Bible	['One Old English Testament']	364.r.11
0	Bible	['one old postell in lattin']	344.r.13a*
0	Bible	['one other in folio plaine roman W^th Com']	342.02c*
0	?Bible	['One Pandectus']	369.r.03
0	Bible	['One Part of the Bible by Jerome']	357.r.03
0	Bible	['One Psalmes in folio']	365.r.02
0	Bible	['One Psalmes in Lattin prose']	360.l.02
0	Bible	['one psalter & one psalmes old']	360.r.13j*
0	Bible	['one psalter & psalmes fillits']	360.l.12h*
0	Bible	['one psalter and psalmes queares']	367.r.03a*
0	Bible	['one psalter in octavo']	368.r.01b*
0	?Bible	['One Robeins Psalmes']	358.r.13
0	?Bible	['One Scriptura Privata']	352.r.04
0	Bible	['one single psalter']	345.r.12f*
0	Bible	['one single psalter']	354.l.03a*
0	Bible	['One Single Testament in 16 ruled Roman']	358.r.15
0	Bible	['one testa & psalmes Clasped']	360.l.12g*
0	Bible	['one Testa & psalmes cross gilt']	360.l.12c*
0	Bible	['one testa & psalmes cross gilt edge']	360.l.12d*
0	Bible	['one testa & psalmes cross ph']	360.l.12f*
0	Bible	['One Testament and Psalmes']	351.l.11
0	Bible	['One Testament and Psalmes in twelve']	358.r.14
0	Bible	['one Testament & psalmes plaine']	345.r.12e*
0	Bible	['one third part of the bible']	359.r.03a*

STC, Adams, or other reference	Author	Title	Davies no.
0	Bible	['One Third part of the Bible, with Testament and Middleborough Psalmes, gilt edge']	358.1.21
cf. 3001.7–13.5	Bible	Psalmes or prayers taken out of holye scripture. 'The King's Psalms'	357.r.15
0	Bible	['Six of psalmes in octavo queares']	366.r.16d*
0	Bible	['ten single test in 8to']	350.1.02k*
2854–54.7	Bible	The first/second tome or volume of the paraphrase of Erasmus vpon the newe testamente	344.1.10
0	Bible	['Three Bookes of the Bible, Lattin']	359.r.20
0	Bible	('three gilt edge english letter')	360.1.13c*
0	Bible	['Three Lattin Testaments']	359.r.08
0	Bible	['three new engl[ish] bost and buft']	345.1.02c*
0	Bible	['three psalmes roman Claspes']	360.1.13e*
0	Bible	['three single Testaments in 16']	359.r.06b*
0	Bible	['twelve bibles cross silvered']	360.r.13i*
0	Bible	['Twenty-two Single Psalters']	366.1.20
0	Bible	['Two Apocraphi of the Bible']	365.r.08
0	Bible	['two [bibles] plaine wth ouills']	345.1.02a*
0	Bible	['two Com & psalmes plaine']	345.r.12d*
0	Bible	['Two David Psalmes']	357.1.15
0	Bible	['two gilt edge roman']	360.1.13f*
0	Bible	['Two Greeke Testamentes']	359.1.15
0	Bible	['two of psalmes']	369.1.01a*
0	Bible	['two psalmes engl[ish] ph Claspes']	360.1.13a*
0	Bible	['two psalmes for Com in quarto q^{res}']	366.r.16b*
0	Bible	['two psalms gilt engl[ish] letter']	360.1.13b*
0	Bible	['two psalmes in four parts']	367.r.03b*

STC, Adams, or other reference	Author	Title	Davies no.
0	Bible	['two psalters & psalmes gilt edge']	360.1.13d*
0	Bible	['two servis & one psalms in large quarto']	366.r.16a*
0	Bible	['two servis & psalmes in small print']	359.r.06d*
Ad B1646	Bible. Apocrypha	Liber Hasmonaeorum qui vulgo Prior Machabaeorum	349.1.10
3022.7–27	Bible. Appendix	The doctrine of the Bible	358.1.12
3023	Bible. Appendix	The doctrine of the Bible	367.1.22
2352	Bible: O.T.: Psalms; Apolinarius	Ἀπολιναρίου μετάφρασις τοῦ ψάλτηρος, διὰ στίχων ἡρωϊκῶν	355.r.04
3053–54.5	Bidpai	The morall philosophie of Doni	363.1.02
3152–57	Blundeville, Thomas	The fower chiefyst offices belongyng to horsemanshippe	366.r.08
cf. 3168–70	Boaistuau, Pierre	Theatrum mundi, the theatre or rule of the world	349.1.03
3228–30	Bolton, Robert	A discourse about the state of true happinesse	365.r.07
3228–30	Bolton, Robert	A discourse about the state of true happinesse	366.r.12
cf. Ad B2364–70	Bolzanius, Urbanus	['One Urbanus Gramer']	369.1.15
3363.9–64	Book	A new booke of spelling with syllables	362.r.02*
?3306	Book	The booke of fortune	369.r.06
cf. 3327.3–47.5	Book	A newe boke of presidentes in maner of a register	367.r.01
?lost	?Borde, Andrew	['Two Docter Boardes Retractive']	365.r.04
3397	Botero, Giovanni	Observations upon the lives of Alexander, Caesar, Scipio	351.r.02
3436–37	Bownd, Nicholas	The doctrine of the sabbath, plainely laid forth	347.1.01
3459–59.7	Boys, John	An exposition of the dominical epistles and gospels . . . The spring-part	348.1.06
3462–62.7	Boys, John	An exposition of the festivall epistles and gospels. The first part	348.1.08
3455–56.7	Boys, John	An exposition of al the principall scriptures used in our English liturgie	348.1.07

STC, Adams, or other reference	Author	Title	Davies no.
3455–56.7	Boys, John	An exposition of al the principall scriptures used in our English liturgie	366.r.01
?3462–63.7	Boys, John	An exposition of the festivall epistles and gospels. The first part; the second part; the third part	365.1.14
cf. 3458–60.8 or 3462–63.7	Boys, John	['One Docter Boys, compleate']	366.r.09
3578	Brathwait, Richard	The poets willow	367.1.23
3747–49	Bright, Timothy	A treatise of melancholie	350.1.09
3756	Brightman, Thomas	The revelation of S. John	354.1.07
3774–74.3	Brinsley, John (the elder)	Sententiae pueriles	367.1.04
3768	Brinsley, John (the elder)	Ludus literarius: or, the grammar schoole	365.1.10
3770b.5–71	Brinsley, John (the elder)	The posing of the parts, or, a most plaine and easie way of examining the accidence	361.1.13
3770b.5–71	Brinsley, John (the elder)	The posing of the parts, or, a most plaine and easie way of examining the accidence	365.1.08
cf. 3773	Brinsley, John (the elder)	Pueriles confabulatiunculae	360.1.15
?3961	Bucanus, Gulielmus	Institutions of christian religion	357.r.08
cf. Ad B3024–37	?Bucer, Martin	['One Buserus Defensu Christi']	365.r.10
4008	Buckland, Ralph	Seaven sparkes of the enkindled soule	358.r.06
cf. 4028–32.3	Bull, Henry	[Christian prayers and holy meditations.]	359.1.03
4093–93.5	Bunny, Edmund	Of the head-corner-stone	343.1.06
4093–93.5	Bunny, Edmund	Of the head-corner-stone	364.r.12
4116–16.5	Burhill, Robert	Contra Martini Becani . . . Controversiam Anglicanam	355.1.03
?4192	Butler, Charles	The feminine monarchie	363.1.05
?cont.	Buxtorfius, J., *senior*	Lexicon Hebraicum	354.1.10
?4323.3	C., W.	<Decimarum> et oblationum tabula	371.1.01
4332–34	Caesar, Caius Julius	C. Julii Caesaris commentarii	359.1.07
4332–34	Caesar, Caius Julius	C. Julii Caesaris commentarii	360.1.07
?4336	Caesar, Caius Julius	['Two Ceasers Comentaries']	348.1.12
cf. Ad C97–100	Caesarius, Joannes (Juliacensis)	['Two Cesarius Logickes']	356.r.08

STC, Adams, or other reference	Author	Title	Davies no.
cf. Ad C97–100	Caesarius, Joannes (Juliacensis)	['One Cesarius Logicke']	360.r.10
cf. Ad C202–25	Calepinus, Ambrosius	Dictionarium	344.l.11
0	?Calvin, Jean	['One Abraham's Faith']	346.l.08
?4372	Calvin, Jean	An admonicion against astrology	370.l.11
?4404–04.5	Calvin, Jean	The comentaries . . . vpon the first epistle of sainct Jhon	344.l.02
?4409	Calvin, Jean	An excellent treatise . . . soule	351.l.09
4415–31	Calvin, Jean	The institution of christian religion	354.r.10
?4424	Calvin, Jean	The institution of christian religion	344.l.13
4496	Camden, William	Annales rerum Anglicarum, et Hibernicarum	343.r.06
4511–13.7	Camden, William	Institutio Graecae grammatices compendiaria	352.l.14
?4511–13.7	Camden, William	Institutio Graecae grammatices compendiaria	366.r.20
cont./BN	Camerarius, Joachim, *senior*	Commentatiuncula non esse ex eventis de consiliis actionibusque hominum pronunciandum de exordio versus Ovidiani	357.l.07*
4558–62.3	Cancellar, James	The alphabet of prayers	359.l.05*
4579–80.5	Canterbury	The cobler of Caunterburie	362.r.04
?cont.	?Capavagius	['One Capavagius in Hypocrates']	357.l.06*
?cont.	Cardanus, Hieronymus	['One Hironimus Cardanus']	356.l.01
4637	Carleton, George	Jurisdiction regall, episcopall, papall	347.l.02
4707.7	Cartwright, Thomas	A treatise of christian religion	345.r.09
4740–46	Casaubon, Isaac	['One Cassabon']	349.l.08
4770–73	Castalio, Sebastian	Dialogorum sacrorum libri quatuor	353.r.18
4782–87	Castiglione, Baldassare	Balthasaris Castilionis comitis De curiali siue aulico libri quatuor	352.r.06
4781	Castiglione, Baldassare	The courtier of count Baldessar Castilio	346.l.01
4859	Cato, Dionysius	Cato translated grammatically	367.l.20
4839.4–59.5	Cato, Dionysius	['One Cato']	360.r.20
4839.4–59.5	Cato, Dionysius	['Three Catoes']	363.l.15

STC, Adams, or other reference	Author	Title	Davies no.
4839.4–59.5	Cato, Dionysius	['Two Catoes']	367.r.18
Ad C1169	Cauliaco, Guido de	Chirurgia	356.r.20
12468–69	Cauliaco, Guido de	The questyonary of cyrurgyens	369.1.17
?lost	Celius Secundus	['One Celius secundus in 3 partes']	344.r.14
?cont.	Chemnisius	['One Chemnisius Hormony, six partes']	347.1.11
?cont./BL	Chrząstowski, Andrzej	Bellum Iesuiticum	345.1.16
4923	Churche, Rooke	An olde thrift newly revived	362.r.08
4923	Churche, Rooke	An olde thrift newly revived	366.1.05
5235.2	Churchyard, Thomas	A generall rehearsall of warres	370.r.03
Ad C1582–83	Chytraeus, David	De lectione historiarum recte instituenda	355.r.07
5263–65	Chytraeus, David	['One Davidis Chitreii']	355.r.03
cf. Ad C1730–1849	Cicero, Marcus Tullius	['One Tullis Philosophi']	357.1.01
cf. Ad C1907–34	Cicero, Marcus Tullius	Epistolarum ad Atticum ad Brutum ad Quintum fratrem libri XX	356.1.13
5265.7–68.3	Cicero, Marcus Tullius	De officiis M. T. Ciceronis libri tres	353.1.09
5265.7–68.3	Cicero, Marcus Tullius	De officiis M. T. Ciceronis libri tres	367.1.05
5266–67.4	Cicero, Marcus Tullius	M. T. Cic. de officiis libri tres	359.r.21
5299–99.8	Cicero, Marcus Tullius	Marci Tullii Ciceronis epistolae ad familiares	359.r.10
?5323.7/Ad C1680	Cicero, Marcus Tullius	Rhetoricorum ad C. Herennium libri quattuor	360.r.05
5318.3–18.7	Cicero, Marcus Tullius	Sententiae Ciceronis, Demosthenis, ac Terentii	356.1.15
5319–20	Cicero, Marcus Tullius	Sententiae Ciceronis, Demosthenis, ac Terentii	359.r.17
?cont.	Cicero, Marcus Tullius	['Twenty Tullii Pro Archia Poeta']	360.r.15
Ad C1694	Cicero, Marcus Tullius	De oratore, Brutus, Orator, de optimo genere oratorum	360.r.08
5308–10.2	Cicero, Marcus Tullius	M. Tullii Ciceronis orationum volumen primum/secundum/tertium	359.1.13
5308–10.2	Cicero, Marcus Tullius	M. Tullii Ciceronis orationum volumen primum/secundum/tertium	368.1.17
cf. 5265.7–68.3	Cicero, Marcus Tullius	['One Tullis Workes']	353.1.12
cf. 5295–307	Cicero, Marcus Tullius	['Foure Tullis Epistles']	353.1.06

STC, Adams, or other reference	Author	Title	Davies no.
cf. 5299–99.8	Cicero, Marcus Tullius	['One Tullis Epistles']	360.1.09
5281–88	Cicero, Marcus Tullius	Marcus Tullius Ciceroes thre bokes of duties	367.1.03
5314.5–15.8	Cicero, Marcus Tullius	Marci Tullii Ciceronis quaestiones Tusculanae	368.r.03
?cont.	?Ciprian	['One Ciprians Greek Gramer']	352.r.05
?cont.	?Ciprian	['Two Cipprians Gramers']	356.1.17
Ad C2054	Claius, Johann	Prosodiae libri tres	351.1.10
5331	Clapham, Henoch	Bibliotheca theologica	349.1.02
5382–87	Cleaver, Robert	A codly form of householde gouernement	352.r.12
Ad C2161–67	Clenardus, Nicolaus	[Hebrew title] Tabula in grammaticen Hebraeam	352.1.12
Ad C2161–67	Clenardus, Nicolaus	[Hebrew title] Tabula in grammaticen Hebraeam	352.r.02
5400.5–04	Clenardus, Nicolaus	Institutiones linguae Graecae	367.r.14
5509–09.5	Coke, Sir Edward	La size part des Reports	344.r.07
5493–94	Coke, Sir Edward	Les reports de Edward Coke (Pt. I)	344.r.06
5511–22	Coke, Sir Edward	La sept/huict^{me}/neuf^{me}/dix^{me}/unz^{me} part des Reports	344.r.08*
5499–500	Coke, Sir Edward	Le tierce part des Reportes	364.1.15
?lost	?Collete	['One Colletes Prayers']	357.r.18
5563	Collins, Samuel	Increpatio Andreae Eudaemono-Johannis	347.1.06
5659	Cooke, Alexander	Pope Joan	362.1.11
?lost	?Cooper	['One Coopers Genologie']	350.1.03
5682–83a	Cooper, Thomas (bishop)	An admonition to the people of England	347.r.02
5686–89	Cooper, Thomas (bishop)	Thesaurus linguae Romanae & Britannicae	369.1.12
5696	Cooper, Thomas (preacher)	The churches deliverance	349.r.04
5711–12	Coote, Edmund	The English schoole-maister	361.r.09
5738–41	Copley, Anthony	Wits fittes and fancies	362.1.01
5759.1–59.4	Cordier, Mathurin	Colloquiorum scholasticorum libri quatuor	353.1.01
5762	Cordier, Mathurin	Corderius dialogues translated grammatically	367.1.02
Ad C2628–30	Cordus, Valerius	?Dispensatorium	360.1.04
5836	Cotta, John	The triall of witch-craft	346.r.05

TC, Adams, or other reference	Author	Title	Davies no.
	?Courtmantian	['One Courtmantian with old prick songes in yt']	361.r.04
912–13	Cowper, William	The anatomie of a christian man	347.l.08
919.5–22.2	Cowper, William	Three heavenly treatises	346.r.08
5961.5	Craig, John	The mother and the child	367.r.23
cont.	Cramer, Daniel	['One Cramerii on Aristotle']	353.r.12
6062–63	Crooke, Helkiah	['One Crooke's Workes whole']	344.r.09
106.3	Culmann, Leonhard	Sententiae pueriles	360.l.16
141.5–48	Curtius Rufus, Quintus	The historie of Quintus Curcius	369.r.20
f.6157–58/18155	Cyprian (saint)	A swete and deuoute sermon	368.r.08
197	Dallington, Sir Robert	Aphorismes civill and militarie	343.r.11
Ad D51–52	Danaeus, Lambertus	Opuscula omnia theologica	344.l.12
Ad D59–60	Danaeus, Lambertus	Politicorum aphorismorum silva	354.r.05
Ad D39–42	Danaeus, Lambertus	['One Daneus Ethickes']	354.r.06
5246–47	Daniel, Samuel	The first part of the historie of England	346.r.13
5258–59	Daniel, Samuel	A panegyrike congratulatorie to the kings maiestie	369.r.13
5288	Darrell, John	A true narration	347.r.03
?lost	Davies, John	The muses sacrifice	358.l.05
6436	Deacon, John	Tobacco tortured	361.r.05
Ad D217–18	Dedekind, Friedrich	Grobianus, et Grobiana	352.l.03
?lost	Deloney, Thomas	The garland of good will	364.l.03
6575.3–75.7	Demosthenes	['One Demostenes Orations']	355.r.02
6575/6576	Demosthenes	['One Demostenes Orations in Greeke']	349.r.01
?6575.3–75.7	Demosthenes	['Three Demostenes Orations']	360.r.18
6649.5–62.3	Dent, Arthur	A sermon of repentance	363.r.09
6622–24.4	Dent, Arthur	A pastime for parents	363.r.12
?6625.3–25.8	Dent, Arthur	A plaine exposition of the articles of our faith	363.r.14f*
6626–30.7	Dent, Arthur	The plaine mans path-way to heaven	353.r.19
6637.5–38	Dent, Arthur	The plaine-mans path-way to heaven. The second part	367.l.24
?6681.5–82	Dering, Edward	A briefe & necessary instruction . . . With Godly private prayers annexed	359.l.04

STC, Adams, or other reference	Author	Title	Davies no.
6681.5–82	Dering, Edward	A briefe & necessary instruction	369.1.01
cf. 6684.5–89.4	Dering, Edward	Godlye priuate praiers	358.r.17
6718–19	Dering, Edward	A shorte catechisme for househoulders	363.r.14b*
6748–53	Desainliens, Claude	The French schoolemaister	367.r.15
cf. Ad D338–67	Despauterius, Johannes	['One Disputerius gramer, in three partes']	349.r.02
0	?Dienetius	['One Dienetius']	369.r.04
6849.5–53	Digges, Leonard	A boke named Tectonicon	362.1.09
?cont.	?Dionysius	['One Dionysio Fonta nona']	356.r.07
?5378–78.2	Dod, John, and Cleaver, Robert	A briefe explanation of the whole booke of the Proverbs	366.r.11
5378–78.2	Dod, John, and Cleaver, Robert	A briefe explanation of the whole booke of the Proverbs	347.1.05
5378–78.2	Dod, John, and Cleaver, Robert	A briefe explanation of the whole booke of the Proverbs	365.1.06
6988	Dodoens, Rembert	Rams little Dodeon	361.1.09
cont./BL	Dominis, Marco Antonio de	De radiis visus et lucis	366.r.04
?cont.	?Domitius Placus	['One Domitii Placi Jesu Theologie']	354.r.14
7027	Donne, John	Ignatius his conclave	368.r.06
7098	Dowland, John	A pilgrimes solace	361.1.01
7091–94	Dowland, John	The first booke of songes	361.1.02
7118	Downame, George	Lectures on the XV. psalme	347.r.11
7140.5–42	Downame, John	A treatise concerning Antichrist	366.1.09
7140.5	Downame, John	Four treatises . . . Whereunto is annexed a treatise of anger	366.1.10
?cont.	?Dradreus	['One Dradreus Loci Comunes']	354.1.03
7174	Draxe, Thomas	Bibliotheca scholastica	353.1.11
7176–78	Draxe, Thomas	Calliepeia	352.1.11
7182	Draxe, Thomas	The christian armorie	368.1.01*
7216–21.5	Drayton, Michael	Poems: by Michaell Draiton esquire	351.r.12
7226–27	Drayton, Michael	Poly-Olbion	365.r.01
Ad D1071	Du Laurens, André	Opera anatomica	354.1.01
?7339–42	Du Moulin, Pierre (the elder)	Theophilus or love divine	357.r.14

TC, Adams, or other reference	Author	Title	Davies no.
?. 7337–37.5	Du Moulin, Pierre (the elder)	['One Moolaines Prayers']	358.r.09
391–92	Dyer, James	La table al lieur des reports	358.r.02
398–401.5	Dyke, Daniel (the elder)	The mystery of selfe-deceiving	365.l.15
408–08.2	Dyke, Daniel (the elder)	Two treatises	365.r.03
474	Eburne, Richard	The two-folde tribute	362.r.01
527.9–30	Egerton, Stephen	A briefe methode of catechising	363.r.14c*
527.9–30	Egerton, Stephen	A briefe methode of catechising	367.r.07
642.7–57	Elyot, Sir Thomas	The castell of helthe	361.l.08
	?Emanuel	['One Emanuell of the Bibles Doctrine']	358.l.19
10049	?England, Church of	['One Articles of Religion']	362.r.03
7722–23.7	England, Local Courts	The order of keeping a court leete	363.l.16
306–14	England, Statutes	A colleccion of all the statutes . . . [ed.] W. Rastell	369.l.13
9526.7–32	?England, Statutes	['One Abstract of the Parlament']	348.r.11
0424–26	Epictetus	The manuell of Epictetus	358.l.04
0424–26	Epictetus	The manuell of Epictetus	368.l.13
	Erasmus, Desiderius	['Twenty-eight bookes of Erasmus, sortes']	357.r.05
Ad E552–68	Erasmus, Desiderius	?Opus de conscribendis epistulis	370.l.14
Ad E789	Erasmus, Desiderius	?Paraphrasis in duas epistolas Pauli ad Corinthios	349.r.10
Ad E539–40	Erasmus, Desiderius	Colloquia	368.r.13
10471.4–73	Erasmus, Desiderius	De copia verborum	369.r.15
cf. Ad E740–44	Erasmus, Desiderius	Paraphrasin in Euangelium Matthaei	369.r.17
0437–41	Erasmus, Desiderius	Prouerbes or adagies	357.r.09
2854–54.5	Erasmus, Desiderius	The first tome or volume of the paraphrase of Erasmus	369.l.06
?10536	?Est, William	The right rule of a religious life	350.r.03
)	Este, Michael	['Three Settes of Eastes']	361.r.02
?Ad E1030–35	Euripides	['One Eurepides in two volumes, Greek']	370.l.08
Ad E1036	Euripides	Hecuba et Iphigenia	369.l.03
?cont.	?Fabrius	['One Fabrij Auscula']	345.l.12
?10769	Fenner, Dudley	Certain godly and learned treatises	350.r.12

STC, Adams, or other reference	Author	Title	Davies no.
?10782.5	Fennor, William	Cornu-copiae, Pasquils night-cap	369.1.04
10787.2–87.4	Fenton, Edward	So short a catechisme	364.r.06
10806–07	Fenton, Roger	A treatise of usurie	366.1.11
?Ad F253	Fernelius Johannes	['One Fernelius Phisickes']	359.1.19
0	Fisher	['One Fishers Book']	370.1.03
?cont.	Fisher, John	['One John Roffensis']	370.1.02
10954–57	Fitzherbert, Sir Anthony	[La graunde abbregement de le ley.]	344.r.05
10978–82	Fitzherbert, Sir Anthony	[Crompton's enlargement in law French.]	348.r.03
?Ad F556–57	Flacius, Mathias	Clauis scripturae	343.1.14
cont./BL	Flaminio, Marco Antonio	['One Fleminii in Psalmas']	360.r.06
11037.3	Fleming, Abraham	[The conduit of comfort. Partly in verse.]	359.1.02
11076–77	Fletcher, Joseph	Christes bloodie sweat	363.1.03
11087	Fletcher, Robert	The nine English worthies	366.r.07
cont./BL	Foglietta, Uberto	De Causis magnitudinis Imperii Turcici	355.r.01
lost	Ford, Emanuel	['One Montillion']	363.r.05
11189	Forset, Edward	A defence of the right of kings	365.1.11
11194–97	Fortescue, Sir John	A learned commendation of the politique lawes of Englande	351.r.15
10638.5–39	?Fotherby, J.	The couenant betweene God and man	367.1.15
11316.5–19	Francis, of Sales (saint)	An introduction to a devoute life	357.r.20
?11328	?Frankfurt Fair	['Twenty-foure Cattaloges of the Martes']	370.r.05
?11328	?Frankfurt Fair	['One Cattolog of the Mart']	363.r.03
Ad F1013	Freigius, Johannes Thomas	Paedagogus	356.r.22
Ad F1017	Freigius, Johannes Thomas	Quaestiones geometricae et stereometricae	356.r.12
11410	Fulbecke, William	A direction or preparative to the study of the lawe	353.r.03
11412–13.7	Fulbecke, William	An historicall collection of the continuall factions, of the Romans and Italians	346.1.04
?5009	?Fulke, D.	A treatise against the Defense of the Censure	368.1.02
?11496–96.3	G., H.	The mirrour of maiestie	361.1.11
11531–37.3/?cont.	Galen	['One Gallaines Phisickes']	370.1.07*

STC, Adams, or other reference	Author	Title	Davies no.
11530–37.3/?cont.	Galen	['One Gallaines Phisickes']	356.l.18
cont./BL	Galen	De Constitutione artis medicae	353.r.07
11554.5–59	Garden	['One Godly Garden']	359.r.04*
11554.5–59	Garden	['one godly garden wth psalms old']	359.r.06e*
11554.5–59	Garden	['Four Godly Gardens']	368.r.15
Ad G372	Gemma, Cornelius	De arte cyclognomica	345.l.10
cf. Ad H1274–82	Gerardus/Hyperius, Andreas	['One Hyperii Theologia']	356.r.01
11760–61	Gerardus/Hyperius, Andreas	A speciall treatise of Gods prouidence	367.l.14
cf. 11755–62 and Ad H1263–82	Gerardus/Hyperius, Andreas	['One Andrea Hyperii']	355.r.10
cf. 11848–48.3	Gifford, George	A catechisme . . . giving a most excellent light to all those that seeke to enter the Pathway to Salvation	368.r.17
1154–56	Gifford, George	Fifteene sermons	350.r.08
11905–06	Glanvilla, Ranulphus de	Tractatus de legibus	351.r.16
11937–38	Godwin, Francis	A catalogue of the bishops of England	347.l.07
0	?Gombart	['One Sett of Gombartes']	361.r.03
12022.7–23	Goodman, Godfrey	The fall of man	345.r.08
0	Grammar	['Four Accidences']	363.r.04
0	Grammar	['foure old lattin gramers']	370.l.07a*
0	Grammar	['One Albanus Grammer']	357.l.05
0	Grammar	['One Gramer with paper in yt']	369.l.20
0	Grammar	['one old gramer']	370.l.13a*
0	Grammar	['one old gramer Construed']	370.l.20a*
0	Grammar	['one old lattin dictionary']	369.l.10a*
0	?Grammar	['One Poetica Lattina Nova']	352.l.08
0	Grammar	['Six Gramers']	353.r.15
0	Grammar	['Three Gramers construed']	367.l.06
0	Grammar	['Twenty-five Accidences']	365.l.12
0	Grammar	['Twenty-five Gramers']	366.l.19
0	Grammar	['Two French Dictionaries']	343.r.08
0	Grammar	['Two Gramers']	368.r.01
12182	Granger, Thomas	Pauls crowne of rejoycing	366.l.17
12185	Granger, Thomas	The tree of good and evill	363.l.13
12285–89	Greene, Robert	Pandosto. The triumph of time	362.l.05

STC, Adams, or other reference	Author	Title	Davies no.
cf. 12291.5	Greene, Robert	The pleasant historie of Dorastus and Fawnia	363.r.06
cf. 12327	?Greenwood, Henry	['Four Greenewoddes Workes']	367.r.03
Ad G1101–03	Gregorius, Petrus	Syntaxes artis mirabilis	360.1.06
cf. 12407–08	Grymeston, Elizabeth	Miscelanea. Meditations. Memoratives	358.1.16
12416.5–20	Guarna, Andreas	Bellum grammaticale nominis & verbi regum	360.r.16
12494	Guild, William	A yong mans inquisition, or triall	350.r.10
cf. 12582.2–82.18	?Habermann, Johann	['One Securitie']	357.r.12
12610	Hakewill, George	An answere to a treatise written by D^r. Carier	345.r.10
12648–48a.5	Hall, Joseph	Characters of vertues and vices: in two bookes	352.r.09
cf. 12650–54	Hall, Joseph	Contemplations upon the principall passages of the holie storie	367.r.16
cf. 12661.7–63.6	Hall, Joseph	['One Halls Decades']	364.1.08
cf. 12661.7–63.6	Hall, Joseph	['One Halls Epistles']	367.1.13
12661.7–62.5	Hall, Joseph	Epistles the first volume: containing II. decads	352.1.04
12671–72	Hall, Joseph	Holy observations. Lib. I.	358.1.17
cf. 12679–83	Hall, Joseph	Meditations and vowes divine and morall	358.1.13
12696–97a	Hall, Joseph	The peace of Rome	348.1.04
?cont.	?Hamelmann, Hermann	['One Hermanus']	369.r.21
0	?Harrington	['One Harrington in foure Evangelists']	369.1.10
12866–68a	Harrison, William (king's preacher)	Deaths advantage little regarded	350.r.07
12866–68a	Harrison, William (king's preacher)	Deaths advantage little regarded	367.r.05
12891	Hart, John (D.D.)	The burning bush, not consumed	367.r.04
12972	Hay, Peter	A vision of Balaams asse	348.1.03
12985–86	Hayward, John (D.D.)	The strong helper	351.1.03
13000	Hayward, Sir John	The lives of the III. Normans, kings of England	346.1.10
cf. 13003.5–06	Hayward, Sir John	The sanctuarie of a troubled soule	357.1.14

STC, Adams, or other reference	Author	Title	Davies no.
cf. 13003.5–06	Hayward, Sir John	The sanctuarie of a troubled soule	368.r.09
13041–45	Heliodorus	An Aethiopian historie written in Greeke . . . Englished by T. Underdoune	370.1.05
13056.5–57	Hemmingsen, Niels	Enchiridion theologicum	356.r.04
cf. 13196–201	Heresbach, Conrad	Foure bookes of husbandry. Newely Englished, and increased by B. Googe	347.r.09
?13213–14	?Herman V (archbishop)	['One Hermans Disputation']	348.r.14
13244	Herring, Francis	Pietas pontificia	362.r.05
13244	Herring, Francis	Pietas pontificia	365.r.15*
13266	Heydon, Christopher	A defence of judiciall astrologie	345.r.15
13388–89	Hieron, Samuel	An answere to a popish ryme	366.1.14
cf. 13406.3–10	Hieron, Samuel	A helpe unto devotion	357.1.22
13455.7–56.5	Higgons, Theophilus	A sermon preached at Pauls Crosse . . . In testimonie of his reunion with the church of England	348.1.13
13485–89	Hill, Thomas (Londoner)	The gardeners labyrinth	361.1.07
cf. Ad H563–75	Hippocrates	['One Hipocrates Phisickes']	369.r.05
?Ad H619	Hippocrates	['One Hurneus in Hipocrates']	349.1.13
?12624–26a	?Häkluyt, Richard	['One Holcottes Workes']	369.r.09
cf. Ad H710–40	Holywood, John (=Johannes de Sacro-Bosco)	['One Johan. de Sacra Bosco']	348.r.09
cf. Ad H792–97	Homer	['One Homer Odises']	359.1.16
cf. Ad H792–94	Homer	['One Homer Odisses, Greek and Lattin']	356.1.21
cf. 13638.5–81.3	Homilies	['One Old Lattin book of Homiles']	356.r.11
cf. 13638.5–81.3	Homilies	['One Homilies']	368.r.07
13702	Hooke, Christopher	The child-birth or womans lecture	346.r.14
13745.5	Hooper, John	A godlie and profitable treatise, conteinyng a declaration of Christe and his office	358.1.18
13778–80	Hopton, Arthur	A concordancy of yeares	353.1.10
13776	Hopton, Arthur	Baculum geodæticum sive viaticum. Or the geodeticall staffe	347.r.07

STC, Adams, or other reference	Author	Title	Davies no.
?13786–86.5	Horatius Flaccus, Quintus	['One Old Horrace']	360.r.09
13784–93a	Horatius Flaccus, Quintus	['Two Horrases']	354.l.02
13790a–93a	Horatius Flaccus, Quintus, ed. J. Bond	Quinti Horatii Flacci poemata	367.l.01
13858	Howard, Henry (earl of Northampton)	A defensative against the poyson	369.l.18
13877.3–77.5	Howes, Thomas	The markes and assurance of salvation	350.r.04
13877.3–77.5	Howes, Thomas	The markes and assurance of salvation	367.r.12
13933–33a	Hull, John	Saint Peters prophesie of these last daies	366.l.06
13938–39	Hull, William	The third worke of mercy	350.l.10
13941	Huloet, Richard	Huloets dictionarie	344.r.11
0	?	['One Humeries Logick']	356.l.07
14010–13.7	Hutchins, Edward	Dauids sling against great Goliah	357.r.11
14014	Hutchins, Edward	Sampsons jawbone against the spiritual Philistine	358.r.08
cf. Ad I150–61	Irenaeus (saint, bishop of Lyons)	['One Ireneus adversus Herises']	354.r.17
?cont.	?Irenius	['One Irenius Hebru Gramer']	352.l.15
cf. 14272	Isocrates	['Nine Isocrates three Orations']	360.l.19
cf. 14308–08.5 and 14315	Jackson, Thomas (dean of Peterborough)	The eternall truth of scriptures . . . Delivered in two bookes of commentaries upon the Apostles Creede	365.r.12
14323–26.3	Jacob (the patriarch)	Thystory of Jacoby and his twelve sones	362.r.07
cf. 14348–55	James I (king of England)	Βασιλικὸν δῶρον	364.l.09
cf. 14390–97.7	James I (king of England)	['Two Kinges Speech']	365.l.04
14426	James I, Appendix	Lucta Jacobi: or, a bonefire for his majesties double deliverie	365.r.14*
14426	James I, Appendix	Lucta Jacobi: or, a bonefire for his majesties double deliverie	366.r.13
Ad J114	Jerome (saint)	Index, per Ioan. Oecolampadium	369.l.05
cf. 14596–99 or 14611	Jewel, John	['One Jewells Sermons']	352.r.10
cf. 14581–95	Jewel, John	['One Jewells Apologie']	369.l.07
?cont.	?Jocam	['One Jocams Logick']	356.r.10
14651.5–54	John XXI (pope)	The treasury of healthe	353.r.06

STC, Adams, or other reference	Author	Title	Davies no.
4665–66	Johnson, Jacobus	Schediasmata poetica; sive epigrammatum libellus	368.r.04
4679–80	Johnson, Richard	The most famous history of the seuen champions of christendome	346.1.03
4751–52	Jonson, Benjamin	The workes of Benjamin Jonson	343.1.02
cf. Ad J358	Josephus, Flavius	['Three Josephus Wares of the Jewes']	354.r.11
?cont.	Junius, Franciscus (senior)	['One Junius on Deutrinomie']	349.r.07
Ad J467	Junius, Franciscus (senior)	Grammatica Hebraeae linguae	346.r.04
cf. 7300–01	Junius, Franciscus (senior)	Sacrorum parallelorum libri tres	354.r.18
Ad J475	Junius, Franciscus (senior)	Libri III. Mosis, qui Leuiticus vulgo inscribitur, analytica explicatio	349.1.12
14889–90	Juvenalis, Decius Junius	Junii Juvenalis et Auli Persii satyrae [ed. T. Farnaby]	350.1.05
cont./BN	Keckermannus, Bartholomaeus	Contemplatio gemina	354.1.15
cf. 14895	Keckermannus, Bartholomaeus	['One Kerkerman's Practices']	344.1.18
?cont./BN	Keckermannus, Bartholomaeus	?Praecognitorum logicorum tractatus III.	354.1.14
14898	Keckermannus, Bartholomaeus	Systema ethicae	354.1.12
cont./BN	Keckermannus, Bartholomaeus	Systema logicae	354.1.13
?cont.	Keckermannus, Bartholomaeus	['One Cursus Keckerman']	354.r.04
?cont.	Keckermannus, Bartholomaeus	Systema physicum, septem libris adornatum	354.r.03
cf. 14920–21	Keltridge, John	['One Keltridge Lectures']	349.r.09
cf. 23973–82.5	Thomas à Kempis	['One Imitation']	357.1.12
cf. 23969–71	Thomas à Kempis	['One Imitation of Christ']	370.1.10
cf. 23973–82.5	Thomas à Kempis	['one Imitation whole ph']	357.1.16a*
?23995–97	Thomas à Kempis	['One Imitation, the fourth part']	358.1.08
14950–52	Kilby, Richard (of Derby)	The burthen of a loaden conscience	351.1.15*
14950–52	Kilby, Richard (of Derby)	The burthen of a loaden conscience	368.1.06

STC, Adams, or other reference	Author	Title	Davies no.
cf. 14954.7	Kilby, Richard (of Derby)	Hallelu-iah: praise yee the Lord, for the unburthening of a leaden conscience	351.r.01*
14959.5–60	Kimedoncius, Jacobus	Of the redemption of mankind	346.r.02
14973	King, Humphrey	An halfe-penny-worth of wit	362.r.06
14976–79	King, John (bishop)	Lectures vpon Jonas	366.l.16
15017–24	Kitchen, John	Le courte leete, et court baron	367.r.08
15017–24	Kitchen, John	Le courte leete, et court baron	370.l.12
?cont.	?Labavius	['Three Labavius Controverses']	356.l.11
15145–59	Lambard, William	The duties of constables	363.r.11
15145–59	Lambard, William	The duties of constables	367.r.09
15163–73	Lambard, William	Eirenarcha: or of the office of the justices of peace	352.r.14
?15163–73	Lambard, William	Eirenarcha: or of the office of the justices of peace	353.r.17
15163–73	Lambard, William	Eirenarcha: or of the office of the justices of peace	357.l.09
cf. 15192	?Lanfrancus (of Milan)	['One Lanfrancke']	356.r.16
cf. 15233–40	La Primaudaye, Pierre de	The French academie	348.l.05
15276–82	Latimer, Hugh	27 sermons preached by the ryght reuerende . . . maister Hugh Latimer	349.r.06
cont./BL	Lauterbach, Joannes (of Noscowitz)	Princeps Christianus	353.l.17
cont./BL	Lauterbach, Joannes (of Noscowitz)	Princeps Christianus	354.r.07
15402	Leigh, Dorothy	The mothers blessing	368.l.11
15416–20	Leigh, Valentine	The moste profitable and commendable science, of surueying	362.r.09
cf. 15433–34	Leighton, William	The teares or lamentations of a sorrowfull soule	358.r.07
15485	Le Petit, Jean François	The Low-Country commonwealth	348.r.07
15491	Lescarbot, Marc	Nova Francia	346.l.07
?cont.	?Lessius, Leonardus	['One Lessia de Justetia Jure']	343.r.09
15541	Lever, Ralph	The arte of reason, rightly termed, witcraft	356.r.22
15564–65	Lewkenor, Sir Lewis	The estate of English fugitiues	370.l.06*
cf. Ad L682–98	Linacre, Thomas	['One Linnacrii Brittaine']	357.l.04
cf. Ad L682–98	Linacre, Thomas	['One Linacrii Brittaina']	355.r.05

STC, Adams, or other reference	Author	Title	Davies no.
15658–65	Lindsay, Sir Dauid	The warkis of the famous and vorthie knicht Schir Dauid Lyndesay	348.1.11
15687.7	Ling, Nicholas	Politeuphuia wits common wealth	358.1.09
cf. 15694–703.5	?Lipsius, Justus	['Two Justius']	353.r.11*
cf. 15750–56	Littleton, Sir Thomas	Les tenures de monsieur Littleton	368.1.09
cf. 15730–81	Littleton, Sir Thomas	['One Litletons Tennures']	351.r.14
cf. 15730–81	Littleton, Sir Thomas	['One Old Litletons Tenures']	352.1.06
cf. 15730–81	Littleton, Sir Thomas	['One Litletons Tenures']	355.1.10
16466–67	Liturgies	The fourme and maner of makyng and consecratyng bishoppes, priestes, and deacons	369.r.08
16624–26	Lloyd, Lodowick	The pilgrimage of princes	347.1.04
16696	Lok, Henry	Ecclesiastes, otherwise called the preacher	349.1.06
0	?Londale	['One Londale contra Ridley']	370.1.01
16805	Lopes, Duarte	A reporte of the kingdome of Congo	348.r.12
?cont./BL	Loyola, Ignatius de	['One Ignatius Instruction']	360.1.10
cf. Ad L1545–48	Lubbertus, Sibrandus	['One Sibrandus Lubertus']	365.r.09
cf. Ad L1545–48	Lubbertus, Sibrandus	['Two Sibrandus Lubartas']	345.1.05
cf. Ad L1607–32	Lucian	['One Lutians Dialoges']	356.r.08
16902	Luis (de Granada)	Granados deuotion	358.1.15
16947–48	Lupton, Thomas	A dream of the deuill, and Diues	363.1.17
cf. Ad L2108	Lycophron	['Two Lycofron, Greeke and Lattin']	352.1.05
17041	Lydiat, Thomas	Emendatio temporum	355.1.09
17175.7–76.7	Macropedius, Georgius	‹Methodus› de conscribendis epistolis	353.1.13
17239.3–39.7 and 17244	Mancinus, Dominicus	Mancinus de quatuor virtutibus	360.1.23
?cont./BL	?Manuel II (Palaeologus)	['One Manuellii Opera']	355.1.12
cf. Ad M427–35	Manuzio, Aldo (the elder)	['One Manutius Gramer']	369.1.19
17278.8–81.5	Manuzio, Aldo (the younger)	Phrases linguae Latinae	351.r.05
17278.8–81.5	Manuzio, Aldo (the younger)	Phrases linguae Latinae	357.1.08
cf. 17278.8–81.5	Manuzio, Aldo (the younger)	Phrases linguae Latinae	359.r.16
17287–89	Manuzio, Paolo	Epistolarum . . . libri x	359.r.07

STC, Adams, or other reference	Author	Title	Davies no.
17287–89	Manuzio, Paolo	Epistolarum . . . libri x	368.1.16
17291–92	Manwood, John	A treatise and discourse of the lawes of the forrest	346.1.05
n	maps	['1 Mapp of Yorkeshire']	370.r.12
n	maps	['12 small Mappes']	370.r.10
17336–37	Markham, Gervase	Cheape and good husbandry	348.1.10
17376–77	Markham, Gervase	Markhams maister-peece	365.1.05
17381–81.5	Markham, Gervase	Markhams methode or epitome	364.1.05
17352	Markham, Gervase	The second and last part of the first booke of the English Arcadia	362.1.10
17409	Marlorat, Augustine	Propheticae, et apostolicae, id est totius diuinae ac canonicae scripturae, thesaurus	343.1.12
17410–11	Marlorat, Augustine	A treatise of the sin against the holy ghost	367.r.25*
17413–18	Marlowe, Christopher	Hero and Leander	362.1.03
17445–47	Marnix van Sant Aldegonde, Philips van	The bee hiue of the Romishe church	355.r.12
cf. Ad M696–713	Martialis, Marcus Valerius	Epigrammaton libri XIIII	359.r.19
17492	Martialis, Marcus Valerius	M. Val. Martialis epigrammaton libri	352.1.16
0	Martiall	['One Martialls Phisickes']	369.1.11
cf. Ad M758, M767–68	Martyr, Peter	['One Peter Marter de euchristi']	355.1.05
Ad M776–79	Martyr, Peter	In duos libros Samuelis commentarii	343.r.14
?Ad M783	Martyr, Peter	Melachim, id est Regum libri duo posteriores cum commentariis P. Martyris et I. Wolphii	343.r.13
Ad M793	Martyr, Peter	Preces sacrae ex Psalmis Dauidis desumptae	360.1.03
17580–85	Mascall, Leonard	The first booke of cattell	345.r.13
17597	Mason, Francis	Of the consecration of the bishops in the church of England	365.1.02
17683a	Mavericke, Radford	Saint Peters watch word	368.r.05
17697.7–98	Maxwell, James	Admirable and notable prophesies	361.1.10
cf. 1783–40	Meriton, George	['One Docter Mirretons Sermon']	366.1.04

STC, Adams, or other reference	Author	Title	Davies no.
17847–47.2	Meung, Jean de	The dodechedron of fortune	346.r.12
17847–47.2	Meung, Jean de	The dodechedron of fortune	366.l.18
17847–47.2	Meung, Jean de	The dodechedron of fortune	366.r.18
?17851	?Mexia, Pedro	['One History of the Empires']	343.r.01
cont./BL	Micyllus, Jacobus	De re metrica	356.r.16
Ad M1579	Moller, Henricus	Enarrationis Psalmorum Dauidis, ex praelectionibus D. Henrici Molleri postrema editio	343.l.13
18041–42	Montaigne, Michel de	The essayes or morall, politike and millitarie discourses	343.r.04
18044	Montemayor, Jorge de	Diana of George of Montemayor	344.l.01
0	?More	['Six Mores Cattachismes']	359.r.03
Ad M1812–15	Mornay, Philippe de	Tractatus de ecclesia	353.r.04
Ad M1812–15	Mornay, Philippe de	Tractatus de ecclesia	355.l.01
18158–61.5	Mornay, Philippe de	A treatise of the church	355.l.13
18140–41.5	Mornay, Philippe de	A discourse of life and death	358.l.06
cf. 18173.5–75.5	Morton, Thomas (bishop)	Apologiae catholicae	347.r.01
18183	Morton, Thomas (bishop)	The encounter against M. Parsons, by a review of his last sober reckoning	349.r.05
18183	Morton, Thomas (bishop)	The encounter against M. Parsons, by a review of his last sober reckoning	365.r.05
?cont.	?Moslaine	['Six Moslaines Figures']	360.r.17
0	Munday	['One Mundayes Philosophie']	357.r.01
18263	Munday, Anthony	A briefe chronicle, of the successe of times, from the creation	351.r.04
cf. Ad M1906 and M1932	Munster, Sebastian	['One Musters Hebru Gramer']	352.r.01
cf. Ad M1906 and M1932	Munster, Sebastian	['One Musters Hebru Gramer']	369.r.14
0	?Murisiadus	['One Murisiadus']	354.r.16
18301	Murrell, John	A daily exercise for ladies and gentlewomen	358.l.07
cf. Ad M2022–28	Musculus, Wolfgang	['One Musculus on John']	344.l.09
cf. Ad M2039, and 18308	Musculus, Wolfgang	['One Musculus Loci Communes']	343.r.02
18354–56a	Napier, John	A plaine discouery of the whole Reuelation of Saint John	350.l.01

STC, Adams, or other reference	Author	Title	Davies no.
18579	Nid, Gervase	Certaine sermons upon divers texts of scripture	364.1.13*
cont./BL	Nizolius, Marius	['One Nissolius Dictionary']	344.1.06
cf. 18617–21	Norden, John	A pensiue mans practise very profitable for all personnes	357.1.17
cf. 18617–21	Norden, John	A pensiue mans practise very profitable for all personnes	357.1.18
18628	Norden, John	A pensive soules delight	358.1.11
18639–40b	Norden, John	The surveyors dialogue	366.1.13
18665–69	Northbrooke, John	Spiritus est. . . . The poore mans garden	350.1.07
cf. 18706a–35	Nowell, Alexander	['Nine Nowells Catachismes']	360.1.17
cf. 18706a–35	Nowell, Alexander	['three nowells Catta']	363.r.14e*
cf. 18701–10a.5	Nowell, Alexander	['One Nowells Cattachismes']	370.r.02
cf. 18707–28	Nowell, Alexander	['One Nowells Cattachisme, Greek and Lattin']	370.1.20*
18773–74	Ockland, Christopher	Anglorum praelia	352.r.07
Ad O98	Oecolampadius, Joannes	Ad B. Pykraimerum, de Eucharistia, responsio posterior	355.1.19
?cont.	?Oefius	['One Oefius on Montanus Phisickes']	344.1.17
Ad O278	Origanus, David	Ephemerides nouae annorum xxxvi, incipientes ab anno 1595	345.1.06
18850	Ormerod, Oliver	The picture of a papist	346.r.01
18866–67	Ortuñez de Calahorra, Diego	The second part of the myrror of knighthood	370.1.04
cf. Ad O369	Osiander, Lucas	?Refutatio scripti satanici a F. Puccio Filidinò in lucem editi	354.r.09
18884–85	Osorio da Fonseca, Jeronimo	Hieronymi Osorii . . . de gloria, libri V	359.r.18
Ad O387–90	Osorio da Fonseca, Jeronimo	De regis institutione et disciplina	352.r.08
cf. 18903.5–11	Overbury, Sir Thomas	A wife, now a widowe	350.1.11
?cont.	Ovidius Naso, Publius	['One Ovid de Artii Amandii']	360.r.07
cf. 18976.4–77	Ovidius Naso, Publius	P. Ouidii Nasonis de tristibus libri quinque	360.1.18
cf. 18951, and Ad S29	Ovidius Naso, Publius	Fabularum Ouidii interpretatio . . ., tradita in academia Regiomontana a G. Sabino	359.1.12

STC, Adams, or other reference	Author	Title	Davies no.
?18947.5	Ovidius Naso, Publius	P. Ouidii Nasonis Fastorum ad Caesarem Germanicum libri sex	360.1.21
cf. 18951–52.3	Ovidius Naso, Publius	['Five Ovid Metamorphises']	353.1.04
cf. 18951–52.3	Ovidius Naso, Publius	['One Ovid Metamorphises']	356.r.03
cf. 18951–52.3	Ovidius Naso, Publius	['One Ovid Metamorphises']	367.1.21
?	Ovidius Naso, Publius	['One Ovides small Workes']	356.r.02
19057–57.3	P., B.	The prentises practise in godlinesse	350.r.06
?Ad P14	Pacius, Julius	In Porphyrii isagogen, et Aristotelis Organum, commentarius	345.1.08
?19088–88.3	Page, Samuel	The allegeance of the cleargie. A sermon	346.r.06
?19101	Pagit, Eusebius	Eusebii Pagetti catechismus Latine aeditus	363.r.14d*
19105.5–07	Pagit, Eusebius	The history of the Bible	357.r.16
19105.5–07	Pagit, Eusebius	The history of the Bible	368.1.12
cf. 19157–59a	Palmerin (de Oliva)	The mirrour of nobilitie	348.1.01
cf. Ad P173–80	Pantaleon, Henricus	['One Pantallian']	360.1.05
n	paper	['18 queares of Copy paper']	371.1.12
n	paper	['4 queares of Duch paper']	371.1.11
n	paper	['1 reame of ruled paper']	371.1.07
n	paper	['6 queares of Damaske paper']	371.1.08
n	paper	['6 queares of Venice paper']	371.1.10
n	paper	['2 queares of Gilt paper']	371.1.09
n	paper	['2 reames of Cordinge paper']	371.1.13
n	paper books	['foure in quarto of two queares A peece']	360.r.21g*
n	paper books	['one of Duch paper two queares']	360.r.21b*
n	paper books	['one of Ruled paper two queares']	360.r.21e*
n	paper books	['one of three queares pott paper in forrell']	360.r.21d*
n	paper books	['one other of Duch paper of two queares & twelve sheetes in vellam']	360.r.21c*
n	paper books	['one paper book in folio 8 q^{rs} Claspes']	344.r.10b*
n	paper books	['one paper booke in folio two queares']	360.r.21j*

STC, Adams, or other reference	Author	Title	Davies no.
n	paper books	['one paper booke of Ryall paper of five queares in forrell']	360.r.21a*
n	paper books	['one parchment book']	344.r.10a*
n	paper books	['seaven paper bookes in quarto wth notes written in them']	360.r.21i*
n	paper books	['three of two queares A peece in narrow folio']	360.r.21f*
n	paper books	['two in quarto of one queare A peece']	360.r.21h*
n	paper books	['two paper bookes']	367.l.18a*
n	paper books	['two paper bookes in lether']	349.r.13a*
n	paper books	['two paper bookes in 8to one ph: one gilt']	350.l.02m*
n	paper books	['two small Coppy bookes']	362.r.10a*
cf. 19179.5–81.7	?Paracelsus	['One Perrasensus']	357.r.02
?lost/cont.	?Pareus, David (or J.)	['Two Perreus on the Corinthians']	345.r.05
?lost/cont.	?Pareus, David (or J.)	['One Perreus on the Hebrues']	345.r.06
?lost/cont.	?Pareus, David (or J.)	['One Perreus ad Romanus']	354.r.02
cf. 19266	Parker, Martin	Robin Conscience, or, conscionable Robin	364.l.02
?19285.2–88	?Parker, Matthew	['100 Degrees of Marriages']	371.r.06
19295	Parkes, Richard	An apologie: of three testimonies of holy Scripture	348.r.02
cf. 19353–74	Parsons, Robert	('One Resolution, first and second part']	358.r.16
19465.7–70.5	Patriarchs	The testaments of the twelue patriarches	367.r.06
Ad P435	Patricius, Franciscus (d. 1597)	Discussionum peripateticarum tomi IV	344.l.05
19511	Peacham, Henry (the younger)	Minerva Britanna, or a garden of heroical devises furnished and adorned with emblemes and impresas of sundry natures	349.l.09
19556–61	Pelegromius, Simon	Synonymorum sylua olim a Simone Pelegromio collecta	352.l.10
19556–61	Pelegromius, Simon	Synonymorum sylua olim a Simone Pelegromio collecta	367.l.10
19640–43	Perkins, John	Here beginneth a verie profitable booke treating of the lawes of this realme	368.l.08

STC, Adams, or other reference	Author	Title	Davies no.
19646	Perkins, William	A golden chaine: or the description of theologie	348.1.09
19697–98	Perkins, William	A discourse of the damned art of witchcraft	352.r.11
19697–98	Perkins, William	A discourse of the damned art of witchcraft	367.1.17
cf. 19709–15a.5	Perkins, William	The foundation of christian religion	350.1.06
cf. 19709–15a.5	Perkins, William	The foundation of christian religion	367.1.18
cf. 19709—15a.5	Perkins, William	['eleaven perkins Cattachismes']	363.r.14a*
19766.5–66.7	Perneby, William	A direction to death	351.1.07
cont./BL	Perotti, Niccolò	['one Cornu Copia']	344.r.12a*
19819–23	Pettie, George	A petite pallace of Pettie his pleasure	362.1.02
19826	Pflacher, Moses	Analysis typica omnium cum veteris tum noui Testamenti librorum historicorum	348.1.02
19853–54	Philips, Edward	Certaine godly and learned sermons	350.r.01
n	pictures	['4 borders of Kings and others']	370.r.18
n	pictures	['6 other Pictures']	370.r.19
n	pictures	['13 Pictures']	370.r.13
cf. 19952–54	Piscator, Johann	['One Piscator on Luke and John']	351.r.07*
?19961–62	Piscator, Johann	['One Piscator on Ramus Schoole']	354.1.08
cf. 19961–62	Piscator, Johann	['One Piscator on Ramus Gramer']	357.1.10
19949–51	Piscator, Johann	Analysis logica euangelii secundum Marcum	351.r.08*
cf. 19955.5–59	Piscator, Johann	Analysis logica Epistolarum Pauli ad Romanos	351.r.09*
19948	Piscator, Johann	Analysis logica euangelii secundum Matthaeum	351.r.06
cont./BN	Pissinius, Sebastianus	De cordis palpitatione	354.1.16
cont./BN	Pissinius, Sebastianus	De cordis palpitatione	356.r.05
19977.7–83	Platt, Sir Hugh	Delightes for ladies	357.1.19
20029–29.5	Plinius Secundus, Caius	The historie of the world	343.1.04
cf. Ad P1564 and P1567	Plinius Secundus, Caius	['One Second part of Pleney in Lattin']	344.1.07

STC, Adams, or other reference	Author	Title	Davies no.
20063	Plutarch	The philosophie, commonlie called, the morals	343.l.07
cont./BN	Polanus, Amandus	Collegium anti-bellarminianum	352.l.07
cf. Ad P1733	Polanus, Amandus	In Danielem prophetam commentarius	354.r.01
cont.	Polyander, John	['One Poliander Respontio']	353.r.01
cont./cf. Ad P1822	Pomerius, Julianus	['One Pomerius de Beata Virgina']	356.l.19
cf. Ad P1987–93	Posselius, Johannes (d. 1591)	['One Posellis Sentaxis']	352.r.03
cf. Ad P1987–93	Posselius, Johannes (d. 1591)	['One Posellis Sentaxsis']	355.r.14
20147.5	Powel, Gabriel	The mysterie of redemption	358.r.03
20148	Powel, Gabriel	Prodromus. A logicall resolution of the I. chap. of the epistle unto the Romanes	350.r.11
?20205.5/?lost	Preservative	['1 reame of unperfect bookes with Preservative against the Plauge']	371.r.08
20203.5–04	Preservative	A godlye and holesome preseruatyue against desperatiō	363.l.10
20203.5–04	Preservative	A godlye and holesome preseruatyue against desperatiō	367.r.13
20306	Price, Gabriel	The laver of the heart	363.l.14
0	?Price, Sir John	['One History of Britaine']	346.l.02
cf. 20373–81	Primer	['three gilt primers']	360.r.11a*
cf. 20373–81	Primer	['one plaine primer']	360.r.11b*
cf. Ad P2181–83 and P2186–87	Prudentius, Aurelius Clemens	['Two Prudentius']	353.l.05
cf. 9547–49	Pulton, F.	A kalender, or table, comprehending the effect of all the statutes untill the end of 3. Jacobi. Whereunto is annexed an abridgement of all the statutes	344.r.04
?cont.	?Qualbergius	['One Qualbergius in Genisis']	355.r.17*
cf. Ad Q47, Q49, Q50	Quintilianus, Marcus Fabius	['One Quintillian Declamationes']	356.r.06
15246–47	Ramus, Petrus	The logike of . . . P. Ramus	370.l.21
cf. Ad R98–100	Ramus, Petrus	Grammatica Graeca, quatenus á Latina differt	369.r.16

STC, Adams, or other reference	Author	Title	Davies no.
cf. Ad R128–30	Ramus, Petrus	['One Ramus Philosophy']	354.r.19
cf. Ad R128–30	Ramus, Petrus	['One Ramus Philosophy']	355.l.15
cf. 15252–53	Ramus, Petrus	['One Ramus Gramer']	353.r.09
cf. 20703.5–15	Rastell, John (barrister and printer)	The exposicions of the termes of the lawes of England	351.r.13
20762.5–63.5	Ravisius, Joannes	Epithetorum Joann. Rauisii Textoris epitome	359.l.18
20762.5–63.5	Ravisius, Joannes	Epithetorum Joann. Rauisii Textoris epitome	368.l.18
cf. 20761.2–61.3	Ravisius, Joannes	Joannis Ravisii Textoris epistolae	359.l.11
cf. 20761.2–61.3	Ravisius, Joannes	Joannis Ravisii Textoris epistolae	368.l.14
20761	Ravisius, Joannes	Joan. Rauisii Textoris Niuernen: dialogi aliquot festiuissimi	359.l.17
20761	Ravisius, Joannes	Joan. Rauisii Textoris Niuernen: dialogi aliquot festiuissimi	368.l.15
20812–14	Record, Robert	The pathway to knowledge	366.r.05
20850–51	Regius, Urbanus	The sermon, which Christ made on the way to Emaus set downe in a dialogue	347.r.04
20850–51	Regius, Urbanus	The sermon, which Christ made on the way to Emaus set downe in a dialogue	366.r.03
20862	Relation	A relation of all matters passed . . . according to the originall of Mercurius Gallo-Belgicus	364.l.07
cf. 20862	Relation	A relation of all matters passed . . . according to the originall of Mercurius Gallo-Belgicus	356.l.04
cf. 20862	Relation	A relation of all matters passed . . . according to the originall of Mercurius Gallo-Belgicus	367.r.24
?cont.	?Renodeus	['One Renodeus']	354.l.09
cf. Ad R417	Reusner, Nicolaus	Symbolorum imperatoriorum classis prima / secunda / tertia	354.l.17
cf. Ad R456–58	Rhodolphus, Caspar	['One Rodulphus Logicke']	357.r.04
21031.5–33	Rider, John	Bibliotheca scholastica. A double dictionarie	345.l.04

STC, Adams, or other reference	Author	Title	Davies no.
21031	Rider, John	A friendly caveat to Irelands catholickes	346.1.13
Ad R560	Ringelbergius, Joachimus Fortius	Lucubrationes, uel potius κυκλοπαίδεια	356.1.10
21074	Roberts, Alexander	A sacred septenarie, or the seven last wordes of our saviour	349.1.04
cf. 21073	Roberts, Alexander	['One Robert on the xxxth Psalme']	361.r.07
cf. 21153–62	Roesslin, Eucharius	The byrthe of mankynde	349.r.13
21204	Rogers, Richard	A commentary upon the whole booke of Judges	343.r.12
21215–18	Rogers, Richard	Seven treatises, containing such direction as is gathered out of the holie scriptures	364.r.13
21237	Rogers, Thomas (M.A.)	An historical dialogue touching antichrist and poperie	364.1.11
cf. 21226–27	Rogers, Thomas (M.A.)	The English creede	365.r.06
21267–68	Rollock, Robert	Analysis dialectica Roberti Rolloci Scoti, in epistolam ad Romanos	355.1.02
21285	Rollock, Robert	Tractatus de vocatione efficaci	355.r.13
21317	Rosa, Thomas	Idaea, sive de Jacobi Magnae Britanniae, regis, virtutibus enarratio	351.r.03
21317	Rosa, Thomas	Idaea, sive de Jacobi Magnae Britanniae, regis, virtutibus enarratio	355.r.15
0	?Rossi	['One Rossi Observatione']	354.1.11
21378	Rowlands, Samuel	The famous historie of Guy earle of Warwick	362.1.04
21378	Rowlands, Samuel	The famous historie of Guy earle of Warwick	366.r.06
?cont.	?Roygny	['One Roygny Confutation']	349.1.07
21446.7	Rule	A right godly rule	358.r.19
cf. 15255–57, and Ad L214–23	Sadeelis, Antonius/La Roche de Chandieu, Antoine de	['One Sadellii']	355.1.16
Ad L212	Sadeelis, Antonius/La Roche de Chandieu, Antoine de	Opera theologica	348.r.01
cf. 21559–80	Saint German, Christopher	['Two Doctor and Student']	368.1.04
cf. 21622.2–23	Sallustius Crispus, Caius	['One Salustus']	353.1.02
cf. Ad S140–49	Sallustius Crispus, Caius	['One Salust with a Coment']	369.r.18

STC, Adams, or other reference	Author	Title	Davies no.
cf. Ad S164, S165	Sallustius Crispus, Caius	['One Salustus']	360.r.01
21713–14	Sandys, Edwin (archbishop)	Sermons made by the most reuerende Edwin, archbishop of Yorke	346.r.10
21713–14	Sandys, Edwin (archbishop)	Sermons made by the most reuerende Edwin, archbishop of Yorke	365.1.07
21726	Sandys, George	A relation of a journey begun An: Dom: 1610. Foure bookes	343.1.03
Ad S597–99	Scaliger, Julius Caesar	Poetices, libri septem	367.1.11
Ad S610–11/?lost	Scapula, Johannes	Lexicon Graecolatinum nouum	343.1.11
21821–21.8	Schonaeus, Cornelius	Terentius christianus	353.1.03
21865–67	Scot, Reginald	A perfite platforme of a hoppe garden	362.r.10
0	?Scott	['Two Scottes Colloqui']	351.1.14
0	?Scott	['One Scottes Concordance in Lattin']	344.r.12
0	?Scott	['One Scottes Inchiredion']	360.1.11
22134.5–37	Seager, Francis	The scoole of vertue	363.1.08
?	?Seale	['Nine Seales Catta: in Lattin']	360.r.19
22164	Segar, Sir William	Honor military, and civill, contained in foure bookes	344.r.10
cf. Ad S892	Seneca, Lucius Annaeus	['Two Senecaes Works']	351.r.11
?	Seneca, Lucius Annaeus	['One Sennicaes Philosophi']	360.r.03
22244–45	Serres, Jean de	A general inventorie of the history of France, unto 1598	344.1.08
22244–45	Serres, Jean de	A general inventorie of the history of France, unto 1598	369.r.02
22250–55	Seton, John	Dialectica breuem in contextum constricta	353.1.14
22250–55	Seton, John	Dialectica breuem in contextum constricta	367.r.21*
22341.5–43	Shakespeare, William	[The passionate pilgrim]	367.r.20
22356–60b	Shakespeare, William	Venus and Adonis	364.r.10
22399	Sheldon, Richard	A survey of the miracles of the church of Rome	347.1.09
22839–39.5	Smith, Samuel (minister in Essex)	Davids blessed man	351.1.02
22841.7–42.5	Smith, Samuel (minister in Essex)	Davids repentance	350.1.04
22874	Smyth, John	The bright morning starre	358.r.10

STC, Adams, or other reference	Author	Title	Davies no.
22877.8–78	Smyth, Richard (preacher)	Munition against mans misery & mortality	358.r.12
22932–33	Sorocold, Thomas	Supplications of saints	357.1.16
22950–52	Southwell, Robert	Marie Magdalens funeral teares	364.r.03
22953	Southwell, Robert	Marie Magdalens funeral teares	361.r.10
22955.7–62	Southwell, Robert	Saint Peters complaint, with other poemes	361.r.06
?22980–82.7, and 22983.5–84.6	Spagnuoli, Baptista	Baptistae Mantuani Carmelitae theologi adolescentia	353.r.16
?22980–82.7, and 22983.5–84.6	Spagnuoli, Baptista	Baptistae Mantuani Carmelitae theologi adolescentia	367.r.17
23039–39.3	Speed, John	The genealogies recorded in the sacred scriptures	366.r.14
23056.5	Speght, James	The christians comfort	363.1.12
23101	Spicer, John	The sale of salt	353.1.16
cf. 23177.5–90	Stanbridge, John	Uocabula magistri stābrigi pri/mū iam edita sua saltē editione	361.r.08
23213–18	Stanford, Sir William	An exposicion of the kinges prerogatiue	362.r.11
cf. 23219–24	Stanford, Sir William	Les plees del coron: diuisees in plusiours titles	346.1.06
cf. 23219–24	Stanford, Sir William	Les plees del coron: diuisees in plusiours titles	369.r.10
23229	Stanyhurst, Richard	Harmonia seu catena dialectica	343.r.05
cf. Ad S1750–95	Stephanus, Henricus	['One Stephinus in Greeke']	345.1.14
?cont.	?Stevartius, Petrus	['One Stevarius ad Corinthios']	348.r.13
cf. 23277.5–78.7, and 23283	Stockwood, John	['Four Stockwoddes Gramers']	353.r.13
23281	Stockwood, John	Progymnasma scholasticum	352.1.02
23315–15.5	Stoughton, Thomas	The dignitie of Gods children	347.r.05
23317/?lost	Stoughton, Thomas	Two profitable treatises: I. Of David's love to the word	365.1.03
cf. 23314	Stoughton, Thomas	The christians sacrifice	357.r.21
?23407, and cf. Ad S1984–85	Sturmius, Joannes	The epistle that Johan Sturmius, . . . sent to the cardynalles and prelates	360.1.22

STC, Adams, or other reference	Author	Title	Davies no.
23422–24	Suetonius Tranquillus, Caius	The historie of twelve caesars	344.1.03
23437–40.7	Susenbrotus, Joannes	Σὺν δὲ θεοὶ μάκαρες. Epitome troporum ac schematum et grammaticorum & rhetorum	360.1.20
23454	Sutcliffe, Matthew	A challenge concerning the romish church	347.r.06
23468	?Sutcliffe, Matthew	The practice, proceedings, and lawes of armes	348.r.04
?23453	Sutcliffe, Matthew	A briefe replie to a certaine odious libel, lately published by a Jesuite	349.r.08
23474–80	Sutton, Christopher	Disce mori	368.r.12
23533–35	Swetnam, Joseph	The araignment of lewde, idle, froward, and unconstant women	362.r.12
?23547–48	Swinburne, Henry	A briefe treatise of testaments and last willes	366.1.15
Ad S2135–36	Sylburgius, Fridericus	Rudimenta graecae linguae	355.r.09
23652–55	Taffin, Jean	Of the markes of the children of God	351.1.04
23830–30.5	Taylor, Thomas	Japhets first publique perswasion into Sems tents: or Peters sermon, preached before Cornelius	345.r.07
23825–25a	Taylor, Thomas	Ἀρχὴν ἁπάντων. . . . A commentarie upon the Epistle to Titus	366.r.15
23873–73.5	Temple, Sir William	Gulielmi Tempelli philosophi Cantabrigiensis epistola de dialectica P. Rami	355.1.14
23870	Temple, Sir William	A logicall analysis of twentie select psalmes	345.r.14
23871	Temple, Sir William	Analysis logica triginta psalmorum	352.1.01
cf. 23885.7–86, and 23888.5	Terentius, Publius	['Six Terrences']	353.1.15
cf. 23885.7–86, and 23888.5	Terentius, Publius	['Eleven Terrences']	366.r.19
23934.2	Themylthorp, Nicholas	The posie of godly prayers	358.1.10
cf. Ad T575–77, and T579	Theophrastus	['One Theophrastus de Causis Plantarum']	356.1.14
cf. Ad T575–76, and T579	Theophrastus	['One Theophrastus de Historia']	355.r.06

STC, Adams, or other reference	Author	Title	Davies no.
23950	Thevet, André	The new found worlde, or Antarctike	346.1.09
Ad T637–39, and T641–42	Thomas (the Irishman)	Flores omnium fere doctorum	359.1.06
24031	Thomson, George	Vindex veritatis. Adversus Iustum Lipsium libri duo	355.1.18
cf. Ad T769–76, and T779	Toletus, Franciscus	['One Tolleti Comentaries']	345.1.15
cf. 24123–24	Topsell, Edward	['One Gesner of four-footed beastes and serpentes']	343.r.07
24124	Topsell, Edward	The historie of serpents	364.1.14
?cont./NUC	Tortellius, Joannes	Commentariorum grammaticorum de orthographia dictionum e graecis tractarum opus	344.r.13
?cont.	Tossanus, Daniel	['One Tossanus on three Evangelistes']	345.r.04
24144–44.5	Tossanus, Daniel	The exercise of the faithfull soule	357.r.10
24190.7–97.5	Treasure	Thys booke is called the Treasure of gladnesse	358.r.18
24281–81a	Trigge, Francis	A touchstone, whereby may easilie be discerned, which is the true catholike faith. Taken out of the epistle of S. Jude	346.r.03
cf. 24287–88.5	Trogus Pompeius	Iustini ex Trogi Pompeij historia, libri .xliiij.	367.r.22*
24313–13.5	Tuke, Thomas	The picture of a true protestant	350.1.08
24314	Tuke, Thomas	The practise of the faithfull	357.r.13
24314	Tuke, Thomas	The practise of the faithfull	357.r.17
24316–16a	Tuke, Thomas	A treatise against paintng	363.r.01
24324–25.5	Turberville, George	The booke of faulconrie or hauking	347.1.03
cf. 24372–89	Tusser, Thomas	['One Tusher's Husbandry']	362.1.06
cf. 24372–89	Tusser, Thomas	['One Tusher's Husbandry']	366.r.02
?24408	?Twyne, Thomas	?The garlande of godly flowers	363.1.11
?24408	?Twyne, Thomas	?The garlande of godly flowers	367.1.19
24409–10	Twyne, Thomas	The garlande of godly flowers	359.r.05*
24409–10	Twyne, Thomas	The garlande of godly flowers	368.r.16*

STC, Adams, or other reference	Author	Title	Davies no.
24421–26	Tymme, Thomas	A silver watch-bell	350.r.05
24494–97	Udall, John	A commentarie vpon the Lamentations of Jeremy	366.1.01
0	unknown	['eighteene bookes in quarto']	363.r.02a*
0	unknown	['Eighteen Old bookes in quarto']	370.r.04
0	unknown	['Eleven Admonetion out of Joell']	364.r.01
0	unknown	['Eleven Booke of Letters']	364.1.12
0	unknown	['Fifteen Sermons in one bundle, of sortes']	363.1.04
0	unknown	['five old bookes in sixteene']	370.1.19b*
0	unknown	['forty four sticht bookes litle works']	363.r.02c*
0	unknown	['Fourteen Old Statutes sticht']	369.r.12
0	unknown	['Ninety-two Old bookes in octavo']	370.1.15
0	unknown	['Nynetene prayers in 32 silvered']	360.r.13h*
0	unknown	['One Age of Man's Lyfe']	367.r.10
0	unknown	['one Baskett of Bookes with some of them perfect and other unperfect with waste paper']	371.r.05a*
0	unknown	['One Booke of Chirurgery in French']	357.1.03
0	unknown	['One Booke of Workes']	363.1.01
0	unknown	['One Book of Predestination']	370.1.19
0	unknown	['one Country Contentment']	361.1.11a*
0	unknown	['One Dapes Ceseronis']	359.1.08
0	unknown	['One Davides Meditations']	357.r.19
0	unknown	['One De conservandii vera beatitudine']	358.r.04
0	unknown	['One De Elocutione Imitasio']	356.r.20
0	unknown	['One De Regno Principale']	353.1.18
0	unknown	['One Diett for the Soule']	364.1.06
0	unknown	['one disputatio bible']	348.r.04a*
0	unknown	['One Duch booke']	353.r.05
0	unknown	['One English booke']	370.r.06

7*

STC, Adams, or other reference	Author	Title	Davies no.
0	unknown	['One Epetomy of Phisicke']	349.1.05
0	unknown	['One Epetomy of Phisicke']	366.1.12
0	unknown	['One Floscull Comon Places']	360.1.08
0	unknown	['One French Eglogues']	360.r.02
0	unknown	['One Greate Serus']	360.r.04
0	unknown	['One Greeke book']	370.r.07
0	unknown	['One Homiliarum Judorii']	355.1.17
0	unknown	['One Kinges Edict']	366.1.02
0	unknown	['One Libellus Sinopticus']	351.1.13
0	unknown	['One Magnum et Universale']	356.r.18
0	unknown	['One Medicine Veterum']	356.1.22
0	unknown	['One Methodus Elloquentia']	355.r.11
0	unknown	['One Minoratie of the Saintes']	367.1.08
0	unknown	['One Morall Discipline in Lattin']	349.1.11
0	unknown	['One Old Duch booke']	355.r.18
0	unknown	['One Opera Poeticarum']	355.1.11
0	unknown	['one other little booke in lattin']	370.1.21a*
0	unknown	['One Perva Volumines']	357.1.02
0	unknown	['One Picture of Christ']	351.1.06
0	unknown	['One Poeta Minores']	359.r.14
0	unknown	['One Rerum Societatae Jesu']	356.1.20
0	unknown	['One Rosary of Prayers']	359.r.02
0	unknown	['One Sermon on the second Psalme']	366.1.07
0	unknown	['One Sivell Law Booke']	369.1.02
0	unknown	['One Statutes Edw. VI. Hen. III. Hen. VIII.']	344.r.03
0	unknown	['One Summa de Exemplis']	351.r.10
0	unknown	['1 Ten Commandments']	370.r.24
0	unknown	['One Tenter belly']	367.1.12
0	unknown	['One Tractatus de secretes Simo']	356.r.14
0	unknown	['One Treatise of the Church']	366.r.10
0	unknown	['One Treatise of True Love']	351.1.05
0	unknown	['ten old stiched bookes in octavo']	370.1.20c*
0	unknown	['ten other in octavo']	370.1.19a*
0	unknown	['10 queares of Ballettes']	371.1.14

STC, Adams, or other reference	Author	Title	Davies no.
0	unknown	['Thirteen Old folio bookes']	369.r.11
0	unknown	['Three Small Poetes']	360.r.12
0	unknown	['threscore sticht bookes little works']	363.r.02b*
0	unknown	['Twelve Books in one bundle Ittalian, Spanish, and French']	370.1.16
0	unknown	['Twenty-four School bookes of sortes, old']	357.r.06
0	unknown	['Twenty-seaven Play bookes, of sortes']	363.1.06
0	unknown	['Two Evordamus']	361.r.11
0	unknown	['Two Flores Poetarum']	359.1.14
0	unknown	['Two Lattin Bookes']	370.r.08
0	unknown	['Two Meditation against Misery']	358.r.05
0	unknown	['Two Resolution, first part']	357.1.21
0	unknown	['Two settes of Ittallian Songes']	361.1.06
0	unknown	['With five of other sortes']	361.r.01
Ad U80	Ursinus, Zacharias	Explicationum catecheticarum absolutum opus totiusque theologiae quasi nouum corpus. D. Parei studio & opera quatuor partibus comprehensum	352.r.13
cf. Ad V33–35	Valentia, Gregorius de	['One Vellentius upon Johannes']	355.1.07*
cf. Ad V110–23	Valerius Maximus	['Two Valerius Maximus']	359.1.10*
Ad V70–72	Valerius, Cornelius	Tabulae totius dialectices	356.1.05
Ad V70–72	Valerius, Cornelius	Tabulae totius dialectices	367.1.07
?cont.	?Valerius	['One Valerius Theologie']	359.1.09
cf. Ad V155–94	?Valla, Laurentius	['One Vallentius Valla']	369.r.19
cf. Ad V156–96	Valla, Laurentius	['One Laurentius Valla']	353.r.02
Ad V352–54/24632	Velcurio, Johannes	Commentarii in vniuersam physicam Aristotelis libri quatuor	356.1.06
Ad V352–54/24632	Velcurio, Johannes	Commentarii in vniuersam physicam Aristotelis libri quatuor	370.1.17
Ad V405	Verepaeus, Simon	Praeceptiones de figuris seu de tropis et schematibus	350.r.02
cf. Ad V404, and ?24653	Verepaeus, Simon	['One Verepeus Gramer']	356.1.12

STC, Adams, or other reference	Author	Title	Davies no.
24677–78	Veron, Jean	A dictionary in Latine and English	369.l.16
cf. 24787–91.7	Virgilius Maro, Publius	['Three Virgills']	353.l.07
cf. 24789–92	Virgilius Maro, Publius	['Three Virgills']	359.r.09*
cf. Ad V523	Virgilius Maro, Publius	['One Meane upon Virgill']	354.l.05
cf. 24846.5–48, 24850–50.3, 24852–54, 24855, 24862–63	Vives, Joannes Ludovicus	['One Laudovicus Vives']	355.l.08*
cf. 24846.5–48, 24850–50.3, 24852–54, 24855, 24862–63	Vives, Joannes Ludovicus	['One Laudaiurus Vives']	353.r.08
cf. 9229	Vorstius, Conrad	['One Conradii Vorstii']	349.l.01
24916–16.3	W., T.	The araignement and execution of the late traytors	348.r.06
24939.5–40	Wake, Sir Isaac	Rex Platonicus	358.r.11
24962	Walker, John	The English pharise	358.r.01
cf. 25202–06	Weelkes, Thomas	['One Wilkes first set']	361.l.03
25256–59.7	Werdmueller, Otto	A spiritual and most precious perle	359.r.01
25256–59.7	Werdmueller, Otto	A spiritual and most precious perle	359.r.06*
25276.3–79.3	West, William	['One West Presidentes, 2nd part']	345.r.03
cf. 25300–02	Whately, William	['One Wheatleyes Sermons']	351.l.12
25318–19.5	Whately, William	The redemption of time	363.r.08
25363	Whitaker, William	Adversus Thomae Stapletoni Anglopapistae . . . Defensionem ecclesiasticae authoritatis duplicatio	344.r.02
25678–78a	Willet, Andrew	An harmonie upon the first booke of Samuel	346.l.12
25679–80	Willet, Andrew	An harmonie upon the first/ second booke of Samuel	343.l.05
?25692	Willet, Andrew	Limbo-mastix: that is, a canvise of Limbus patrum . . . Containing also a briefe replie to [19296]	346.l.11
25698–99a	Willet, Andrew	Synopsis papismi, that is, a generall viewe of papistry	343.l.08
25755–57	Willoby, Henry	Willobie his Auisa	362.l.08
?25759	?Willoughbie, John	?Mnemosynon Kyrio-euchariston: a treatise on the supper of the Lord	366.l.08

STC, Adams, or other reference	Author	Title	Davies no.
25799–806	Wilson, Thomas (secretary of state)	The arte of rhetorique	349.r.12
25799–806	Wilson, Thomas (secretary of state)	The arte of rhetorique	361.1.12
25786–87	Wilson, Thomas (divine)	A christian dictionarie	365.1.13
?cont.	?Winckelmannus, Johannes	['One Wicklemans de Jesu Christi']	354.r.08
25862–66	Wirsung, Christoph	Praxis medicinae vniuersalis	343.r.10
25884–86	Withals, John	A dictionarie in English and Latine for children	352.1.13
25884–86	Withals, John	A dictionarie in English and Latine for children	367.1.09
25920–22	Wither, George (poet)	The shepherds hunting	364.1.04
cf. 25890/?lost	Wither, George (poet)	['One Withers Workes']	350.r.13
?Ad W240	Wolf, Johannes	Nehemias, siue in Nehemiae de instaurata Hierosolyma librum, commentariorum libri tres	344.1.14
Ad W259	Wotton, Edward	De differentiis animalium	344.1.04
cf. 26049.2–50.12	Writing Tables	['seaven paire of little tables gilt']	360.14b*
cf. 26049.2–50.12	Writing Tables	['thirty one pair of number thre']	360.14d*
cf. 26049.2–50.12	Writing Tables	['three paire dull gilt beste sorte']	360.14a*
cf. 26049.2–50.12	Writing Tables	['twenty of the least sorte']	360.14e*
cf. 26049.2–50.12	Writing Tables	['twenty three paire of large white Tables']	360.14c*
26058	Wylshman, Walter	The sincere preacher	363.1.09*
?cont./BL	?Yūhannā ibn Māsaiwaih	['One Johanes Mesu Opera Devina']	344.1.15
?26098.5	York (city of)	['10 queares of Youle in Yorke']	371.r.07
26105	Youll, Henry	Canzonets to three voyces newly composed	361.1.04
?Ad Z2	Zabarella, Jacobus	Opera logica	345.1.09
?cont.	?Zeggidine	['One Zeggidines Tables']	347.r.10
n		['Claspes, Bosses, and Nayles']	370.r.23
n		['8 pound of soft wax']	370.r.17
n		['15 Sheepe Skins Tan'd']	371.1.04
n		['5 dozen of wodd seales']	371.r.01
n		['4 dozen of Pensheathes']	371.1.02

STC, Adams, or other reference	Author	Title	Davies no.
n		['Inckhornes with Dust-boxes, and standages with other old Inckhornes']	370.r.22
n		['In hustements']	371.r.10
n		['9 paire of band-box bordes in octavo and sixteen']	371.r.09
n		['1 dozen of Forrells']	370.r.11
n		['1 dozen of knot seales']	371.r.02
n		['1 dozen of Spectacle-cases with other old cases']	371.1.03
n		['1 dozen of Vellams']	370.r.09
n		['one forme of wainscott']	371.r.04c*
n		['Pressinge bordes and backing bordes']	371.r.04
n		['7½ pound of hard wax']	370.r.16
n		['shelves in the kitchinge']	371.r.04a*
n		['shelves in the wairehouse']	371.r.04b*
n		['6 gallaines of Incke']	370.r.21
n		['3 dozen and 4 paire of green glass']	370.r.15
n		['3 Dryfattes with shaiuns']	371.r.03
n		['300 Paistebordes']	370.1.22
n		['3 Redd Sheepe Skins']	371.1.05
n		['21 paire of Christall Spectacles']	370.r.14
n		['2 black boxes in folio and 1 in octavo']	371.r.05
n		['2 bunches of Scales with others']	370.r.20
n		['Workinge tooles, as Rowles, Riglittes, Presses with plough hammers, beating Stone, with two Paire of Mooles']	371.1.06

APPENDIX 3

John Foster's Appraisers and Debtors

The identification of Foster's appraisers and debtors given below ranges from the possible to the certain. Without the active advice and help of Bernard Barr, librarian of York Minster Library, many of these names would have remained unidentified.

Where the appraisers give no town or village for Foster's debtors, it has been assumed that they lived in York, or had strong York connections. However, it is possible that this was not always the case.

The following abbreviations have been used in this appendix:

BHI	Borthwick Institute of Historical Research, University of York
DNB	*Dictionary of National Biography*
Foster	Joseph Foster (ed.), *Alumni Oxonienses: the members of the University of Oxford, 1500–1714*, 4 vols. (Oxford, 1891/92)
Register	F. Collins (ed.), *Register of the Freemen of the City of York from the City Records vol. II 1559–1759*, The Publications of the Surtees Society, 102 for 1899 (Durham, 1900)
Registers of St. Michael le Belfrey	F. Collins (ed.), *The Registers of St. Michael le Belfrey, York, Part I 1565–1653*, The Publications of the Yorkshire Parish Register Society, 1 for 1899 (York, 1899)
Skaife, 'Civic Officials'	Robert H. Skaife, 'Manuscript of Civic Officials', 3 vols., microfilm copy, YCA
Venn	John and J. A. Venn, *Alumni Cantabrigienses . . . (Part I: From the earliest times to 1751)*, 4 vols. (Cambridge, 1922–27)
Visitation	Joseph Foster, *Visitation of York made in the Year 1584/85 . . . and 1612* (London, 1875)
YAS RS	The Yorkshire Archaeological Society, Record Series
YCA	York City Archives
YML	York Minster Library

a) **Appraisers**

1. John Bousfield.   Draper, admitted freeman 1581; chamberlain of York 1589; sheriff 1600/01. (See Robert H. Skaife's single-volume 'Manuscript of Civic Officials' (1895), on deposit, YCA: Skaife dates Bousfield's freedom 1582, but see *Register*, pp. 23, 30. No entry is given in the three-volume manuscript version of Skaife, 'Civic Officials'.)

2. William Blanchard.   A 'William Blauncharde stationer' began renting a house and two shops in the 'minster garth' in 1619 (YML, Chamberlain's Rolls, E.1/125); he is probably the 'William Blanchard' who had John Standeven, senior, placed in his custody for recusancy by the ecclesiastical court in January 1607 (J. C. H. Aveling, *Catholic Recusancy in the City of York 1558–1791*, Catholic Record Society Publications, Monograph Series volume 2 (London, 1970), p. 231). William Blanchard married Ann Beeston 9 May 1613, and had two children: his wife was buried 24 April 1623 (*Registers of St. Michael le Belfrey*, pp. 123, 124, 126, 127, 151, 156). Foster's inventory records the lease of a stable partly 'in Willm Blanchard yard'. Skaife, 'Civic Officials', gives a pedigree of the family: one of Blanchard's eighteenth-century descendants was William Blanshard, printer and newspaper owner. The seventeenth-century William Blanchard may have been related to William Blainchard (Blanchard), London stationer 1613–31, freed 1609, whose one recorded apprentice (bound 1610) came from 'Whasse' in Yorkshire (see *STC*, and D. F. McKenzie, *Stationers' Company Apprentices 1605–40* (Charlottesville, Va., 1961), nos. 2739 and 792).

3. Thomas Haton.   Possibly Thomas Hayton, milliner, freed by patrimony 1605. His son, William, a goldsmith, was freed by patrimony in 1616/17 (*Register*, pp. 54, 68). A Thomas Haiton, parchmentmaker, son of William, 'cordiner', was freed by patrimony in 1618/19 (*Register*, p. 70). A less likely candidate is Thomas Huton, 'tapitour' (tapestry weaver), freed by patrimony in 1571/72 (*Register*, p. 14).

4. William Setterthwayte.   William Satterthwaite, tailor, freed 1614/15; chamberlain of York 1627/28 (*Register*, pp. 64, 77).

5. Gilbert Storke.   On 31 August 1614 the lord mayor's court gave 'Gilbert Stork Stationer' the right to pursue his trade in the city for one year (YCA, House Books, vol. 34, fo. 40ᵃ). Davies speculates that Storke was 'an experienced stationer, probably from London . . .' (*A Memoir of the York Press with Notices of Authors, Printers, and Stationers in the Sixteenth, Seventeenth, and Eighteenth Centuries* (London, 1868; reprinted York, 1988, with introduction by Bernard Barr), p. 342n.). Storke's son John was baptized 10 March 1615 in St. Michael le Belfrey, York (*Registers of St. Michael le Belfrey*, p. 128). His son was buried 25 August 1615 and his wife 21 May 1616 (R. B. Cook (ed.), *The Parish Registers of Holy Trinity Church, Goodramgate, York, 1573–1812*, The Publications of the Yorkshire Parish Register Society, 41 for 1911 (York, 1911), pp. 60–62). Bernard Barr suggests that he may be from another trade or a guild other than the Stationers, perhaps the Drapers.

b) Debtors

1. Mr. Dunwell of Wetherby. Probably Matthew Dunwell, vicar of Collingham 1618–61 (see G. E. Kirk, *A Short History of the Parish Church of St. Oswald, Collingham, Yorkshire* (Leeds, 1937), pp. 17, 31). Collingham is a couple of miles from Wetherby. His will, proved 3 January 1661/62, makes the following bequest: 'I give & bequeath unto my son Theophilus Dunwell all my bookes, instruments & my deske that are in my study . . .'. No books are mentioned in the inventory (worth £66 6s. 10d.), but there may be a missing page judging by the arithmetic (BHI, Exchequer Probate Records, York City Deanery, July 1610). For the birth and marriage of his children see Elisabeth Exwood (ed.), *The Parish Register of Collingham 1579–1837*, The Yorkshire Archaeological Society Parish Register Section, 141 for 1976 (Leeds, 1978). Less likely is Richard Dunwell, minister of St. Mary, Bishophill Junior, York, who was charged in 1647 with using the Book of Common Prayer when it was banned by Parliament (James Raine (ed.), *Depositions from the Castle of York relating to the Offences committed in the Northern Counties in the Seventeenth Century*, The Publications of the Surtees Society, 40 for 1861 (Durham, 1861), pp. 9–10).

2. Edward Secker. Edward Secker was freed by patrimony by Richard Secker, 'Cordiner', in 1602 (*Register*, p. 48). Edward Secker, 'Vintner', was chosen a member of the Common Council on 15 January 1614 (YCA, House Books, vol. 34, fo. 47ᵇ). Another Edward Seckar, yeoman of Dewsbury, died in 1622 (*Index of Wills in the York Registry A.D. 1620 to 1627*, YAS RS, 32 for 1902 (Leeds, 1902), p. 81). The former is a more likely candidate.

3. George Townson. Unidentified.

4. Mr. Wilson Attorney. Unidentified.

5. Mr. Claphamson. Robert Claphamson, notary public, buried St. Martin's, York, 1635 (Coney St. or Micklegate?) (*Index of Wills in the York Registry A.D. 1627 to 1636. Administrations A.D., 1627 to 1652*, YAS RS, 35 for 1905 (Leeds, 1905), p. 17). His will, proved 15 May 1635, makes no mention of books (BHI, Probate Registers, vol. 42, fo. 509). Claphamson was appointed a supervisor of Anthony Foster's will in 1610, which he also witnessed; in 1613 he was both witness and supervisor of the will of Foster's wife, Margaret (see pp. 20, 106, 108).

6. Mr. Staveley. Unidentified.

7. Mr. Slator. Unidentified.

8. Mr. Millington his Cussen. Thomas Millington of York, gentleman, died 1623/24 (*Index of Wills in the York Registry A.D. 1620 to 1627*, YAS RS, 32 for 1902 (Leeds, 1902), p. 63). His will, proved 12 April 1624, makes no mention of books (BHI, Probate Registers, vol. 38, fo. 47). Less likely in view of 'Mr.' is Edward Millinton, 'inholder', who was freed in 1593/94 (*Register*, p. 38).

9. Mr. Squier. Thomas Squire, Christ's College, Cambridge, B.A. 1608/09, M.A. 1613; vicar of Escrick 1613–63. Squire was a public preacher at the Minster, and married Elizabeth, the daughter of John Scott, dean of York. His children were baptized at St. Michael le Belfrey. In 1627 he was alleged to hold overly Protestant views (R. A. Marchant, *The Puritans and the Church Courts in the Diocese of York 1560–1642* (London, 1960), pp. 280–81, and G. E. Aylmer and Reginald Cant, *A History of York Minster* (Oxford, 1977) p. 211). (Venn in error says he was buried in 1622.)

10. Mr. Leake.   Richard Leake, St. Catherine's College, Cambridge, B.A. 1588/89, M.A. 1595. Possibly prebend of York 1617–42 (Venn).

11. Mr. Jagure.   William Jagure or Jagger, vicar of Kirkby cum Broughton in Cleveland; died (as Jagure) in 1627/28 (J. Charlesworth and A. V. Hudson (eds.), *Index of the Wills and Administrations entered in the Registers of the Archbishops at York, being Consistory Wills, &c., A.D. 1316 to A.D. 1822, known as the Archbishops' Wills*, YAS RS, 93 for 1936 (Leeds, 1937), p. 41). Instituted 1592 (as Jagger) (John Graves, *The History of Cleveland . . .* (Carlisle, 1808), p. 241). His will, proved 13 November 1627, makes no mention of books (BHI, Exchequer Probate Records, York City Deanery, July 1610).

12. Mr. Fairebanke of thirlebery.   Probably Robert Firbanke of Thirkleby, who, Torr reports, died in 1622 (lost *sede vacante* Probate Register, fo. 522, cited by James Torr, 'Archdeaconry of Cleveland', p. 586 (MS in York Minster Library: information from Bernard Barr)). He was buried in the parish church beside his wife. Matriculated sizar Trinity College, Cambridge, 1551, B.A. 1553/54, M.A. 1557, fellow 1555, ordained subdeacon of Norwell, 1555. Vicar of Thirkleby from 1584 (Venn). His will, proved 16 April 1624 and witnessed 15 February 1621, makes no mention of books (BHI, Probate Registers, vol. 31, fo. 222).

13. Mr. Williamson sadler.   'Petri Willmson sadler' freed two of his sons, Johannes as a saddler in 1604, and Thomas as a vintner in 1618/19 (*Register*, pp. 51, 70).

14. Mr. Thomas Williamson.   Perhaps son of the preceding (see above).

15. Mr. Walter.   Unidentified.

16. Mr. Bubwith of Rothwell.   Richard Bubwith, St. John's College, Cambridge, B.A. 1583/84, M.A. 1587. Rector of Ackworth and rector of Rothwell, 1591–1627. Died 10 July 1627 (Venn). T. D. Whitaker, *Loides and Elmete* (Leeds and Wakefield, 1816), p. 247, states that he was rector of Ackworth and Rothwell. His will, dated 2 July 1627 and proved 18 January 1628, makes specific directions about some of his books. 'I give and bequeath unto my sonne in lawe Willm Stables one Booke entituled the Actes and monuments Item I give and bequeath unto my eldest sonne Richard Bubwith the second pte of holling^s heade cronacle Item I give unto my sonne in lawe Gilberte Cowper the first pte of hollinges heade Cronacle Item I give unto my seconde sonne Samuel Bubwith the rest of my bookes not formerlye bequeathed, he payinge for the same the halfe value they shall be prized unto, at ye direction of my Supervisors hereafter notified and appoynted' (BHI, Probate Registers, vol. 31, fo. 262).

17. Mr. Cooke my Lord Presidents Chaplin.   Alexander Cooke (1564–1632), vicar of Leeds, author and anti-Catholic (*DNB*). Brasenose College, Oxford, B.A. 1585,

B.D. 1596 (Foster). Edmond, Lord Sheffield (later earl of Mulgrave), was lord president of the Council of the North 1606–19 (see R. R. Reid, *The King's Council in the North* (London, 1921; rptd. Wakefield, 1975), p. 488). His will, proved 9 January 1636, is dominated by the disposition of his considerable library, which he thought was worth £100 (see pp. 19, 21, and J. Barnard, 'A Puritan controversialist and his books: the will of Alexander Cooke (1564–1632)', *The Papers of the Bibliographical Society of America*, 86 (1992), 82–86).

18. Mr. Smyth my Lord Presidents Chaplin. Henry Smith matriculated from Trinity College, Cambridge, in 1587. He was probably vicar of Kellington, Yorkshire (1597–1606), and rector of Hemsworth (1606–11) and prebend of York (1613–15) (Venn). Confirmation that he was prebend is found in John Le Neve, *Fasti Ecclesiae Anglicanae 1541–1857. IV York Diocese*, ed. J. M. Horne and D. M. Smith (compilers) (London, 1975), pp. 27–28. Lady Margaret Hoby commented on his preaching in York Minster in 1600 (G. E. Aylmer and Reginald Cant, op. cit. (item 9), p. 209).

19. Mr. Greenewoode. A Charles Greenwood, gentleman, of Yorkshire, attended University College, Oxford, B.A. 1595/96, M.A. 1598, rector of Thornhill, Yorkshire, 1613. However, Thornhill is near Dewsbury, and the absence of a place-name in the manuscript suggests that the inventory's Mr. Greenwood was resident in York.

20. Daniell Bell. Unidentified.

21. Mr. Standeven. John Standeven, vintner, freed by patrimony 1592, chamberlain of York 1594, sheriff 1608/09, died intestate, administration granted 12 September 1623 (Skaife, 'Civic Officials'). The Standevens were a recusant family. In January 1607 the ecclesiastical courts committed John Standeven, senior, to the custody of a William Blanchard, and in March 1608 he was still confined to his son's house (J. C. H. Aveling, op. cit. (p. 98, item 2), pp. 230, 231, and passim).

22. Mr. Greene of Heslington. William Grene of Clare Hall, Cambridge, M.A. 1579, was prebend of York 1588–1640. He died as vicar of South Kirkby, Yorkshire, where he was instituted in 1601 (Venn, and John Le Neve, op. cit. (item 18), p. 33).

23. Mr. Bankes of Horton. Unidentified. Either Horton-in-Ribblesdale or Horton near Bradford. Bernard Barr thinks the entry may be an error for Brooksbanks, a prominent family near Bradford at this time (see William Cudworth, *Rambles round Horton: historical, topographical and descriptive* (Bradford, 1886), pp. 177–80).

24. Sir Edward Stanapp. Sir Edward Stanhope, high sheriff of Yorkshire 1615, buried Kirby Wharfe 1646. The best pedigree is in J. W. Clay (ed.), *Dugdale's Visitation of Yorkshire . . . with additions* (Exeter, 1899), I, pp. 219–24. According to Venn, *DNB* and Foster confuse him with his brother, also Sir Edward (d. 1608). His father, Sir Edward, member of the Council of the North, died in 1603.

25. Mr. Willm Best. A William Best married Margaret Lambton of Malton at some time before 1584 (*Visitation*, p. 182).

26. Mr. Sandwith. Either Thomas Sandwith or his son Henry, appointed jointly (1613–25) as deputies to Edward Bee, keeper of His Majesty's Evidences at York.

Roger Dodsworth described Thomas Sandwith as 'My cosen'. Thomas Sandwith (1561–1634) was also an official of the Council of the North, and lived in Marygate. See B. A. English and C. B. L. Barr, 'The records formerly in St. Mary's Tower, York, Parts I–III', *Yorkshire Archaeological Journal*, 42 for 1967–70 (1971), 198–235, 359–86, 465–518. There is no record of either having attended university.

27. Robert Walmsley. A 'Rogerus Walmeslay, marchant' was made a freeman in 1568 (*Register*, p. 10).

28. Doctor Bankes. Henry Bankes, whose will, which makes no mention of books, was proved 20 June 1633 (BHI, Dean and Chapter, Original Wills, 1633). His will begins 'I Henrye Bankes Doctor and Devinitie and parson of Settrington', identifying him as Henry Banks, Christ's College, Cambridge, B.A. 1580/81, incorporated Oxford, M.A. 1583, D.D. 1608, rector of Scrayingham 1592, rector of Settrington 1599, canon of York 1595, precentor 1613, prebend of Southwell 1613 (Foster). (Foster mistakenly reports that he died before 27 August 1617.)

29. Mr. Sadler. Rector of Holy Trinity, Goodramgate, 1605–? (William Drake, *Eboracum: or the history and antiquities of the city of York* . . . (London, 1736), p. 317).

30. Mr. Cockson. Rev. William Cockson of York died 1631 (F. Collins (ed.), *Index of Wills, etc., from the Dean and Chapter's Court at York A.D. 1321 to 1636; with Appendix of Original Wills A.D. 1524 to 1724*, YAS RS, 38 for 1907 (Leeds, 1907), p. 15). He was rector of St. Crux, York, 1584–94 (Drake, op. cit. (item 29), p. 297), vicar of Ilkley 1595–98 (Robert Collyer and J. Horsfall Turner, *Ilkley: ancient and modern* (Otley, 1885), p. 158), and rector of St. Saviour's, York, 1591–1631 (Drake, op. cit. (item 29), p. 311). His will, proved 16 June 1631, mentions no books, but the inventory of his belongings records 'Books 20 vallew — 2^{li}', as being 'In the Chamber w^{thin} the Studie Chambre' (BHI, Exchequer Probate Records, York City Deanery, July 1610).

31. Mr. John Watt of Thearne. Unidentified. Thearne, Humberside, may be intended. Bernard Barr suggests Thorne, S. Yorks.

32. Mr. Smythson draper. William Smythson, draper, chamberlain in 1598, freed by patrimony 1592/93, master of the Tailors' and Drapers' Company in 1599 and 1615, buried in St. Michael le Belfrey 28 December 1618 (Skaife, 'Civic Officials', p. 694, *Register*, p. 36). His will, proved 8 November 1619, makes no mention of books (BHI, Probate Registers, vol. 35, fo. 498).

33. Mr. Walker of Stillingflete. Edmund Walker, vicar of Stillingfleet 1582/83–1617, buried in the churchyard there near his wife (James Torr, op. cit. (item 12), pp. 392, 395). His will, proved 19 December 1617, contains the following bequests: 'Item I give to my Cosen Mr Roger Lowde one Zuingli Bible. It I give to my Cozen Giles Parker . . . such a booke as my Cozen Mr Roger Lowde will appoint unto him' (BHI, Probate Registers, vol. 31, fo. 190).

34. Mr. Smith of Caruerley. James Smyth was vicar of Calverley 1612–27 (Henry Stapleton, *Memorials of Calverley Parish Church* . . . (Leeds, [n.d., but after 1902]),

p. 142). He took a B.A. from Clare Hall, Cambridge, in 1606/07 (Venn). His will, proved 5 August 1628, makes no mention of books (BHI, Probate Registers, vol. 31, fo. 264).

35. Mr. Hickson.   There were a few Hicksons in York, though Thomas Hingston, vicar choral of York Minster from 1590 who died in 1619/20 and is buried in St. Olave's, may be meant (F. Harrison and W. J. Kaye (eds.), *The Parish Register of St. Olave York Part 1 (1538–1644)*, The Publications of the Yorkshire Parish Register Society, 73 for 1923 (York, 1923), p. 84).

36. Mr. Wade.   Christopher Wade, gentleman, chamberlain of York 1618; sheriff 1619/20; died 29 September 1623 according to Skaife, 'Civic Officials'. However, the will of Christopher Wayde, gentleman, York, proved [3 August] 1625, is possibly his (BHI, Exchequer Probate Records, York City Deanery, July 1610). It makes no mention of books.

37. Mr. Leng of Strensall.   Thomas Leng was vicar of Strensall 1606–31 according to the church guide published *c.* 1971. Strangely, Torr ('Peculiars' (MS in YML), p. 602) gives the vicar for these years as Henry Bancks M.A., referring to D and C Chapter Acts 1565–1684, H4, fo. 413r.

38. Mr. Dodsworth.   Probably Matthew Dodsworth, matriculated St. John's College, Cambridge, 1565, LL.B. 1573. Chancellor to Tobie Matthew, archbishop of York. Lived in St. Belfrey's, York. Died *c.* 1628 (Venn). Father of Roger Dodsworth (*DNB*).

39. George Dickinson.   Probably George Dickinson, alderman, who was engaged in a substantial export trade 1609–33: see Barbara M. Wilson, 'The Corporation of the City of York, 1580–1660', M. Phil. thesis (University of York, 1967), pp. 313–21. A 'George Dycconson, draper' freed his son John, also a draper, by patrimony in 1575/76, and John in turn freed 'Georgius Dickonson, haberdasher' in 1611 (*Register*, pp. 17, 60).

40. Tomisin Watterworth.   'Thomyson Watterworth', daughter to Lowrance W., baptized 22 July 1589, married Ferdinando Robinson 11 November 1616, buried as widow 10 January 1643 (*Registers of St. Michael le Belfrey*, pp. 62, 131, 215).

41. Mr. Sanderson.   Perhaps William Sanderson (or Saunderson), rector of Thorpe Bassett, East Riding, 1605–25. Died 1625/26. (See N. A. H. Lawrence (ed.), *Fasti Parochiales Vol. V: Deanery of Buckrose*, YAS RS, 143 for 1983 (Leeds, 1985), p. 56, E. W. Crossley (ed.), *Index of the Original Documents in the Consistory Court of York A.D. 1427 to A.D. 1658 and also of the Probate and Administration Acts in the Court of the Dean of York, A.D. 1604 to A.D. 1722*, YAS RS, 73 for 1928 (Leeds, 1928), p. 23, and J. Charlesworth and A. V. Hudson (eds.), op. cit. (item 11), p. 64.) The first legacy in his will, dated 22 March 1624, reads: 'I give to my sonne Henry Remmington all my Bookes, my best gowne, and my best cloake' (BHI, Exchequer Probate Records, York City Deanery, July 1610).

42. Tristram Britton.   'Tristram Bryttain, imbroderer', son of a skinner, was freed by patrimony in 1587/88. He freed his son, Robert, into his own trade in 1613/14, and another son, William, in 1624/25 (*Register*, pp. 30, 63, 75).

43. Mr. Belwodd.   Roger Bellwood, Trinity College, Cambridge, B.A. 1597/98, M.A. 1601, vicar of St. Crux, York, 1609–23. Buried there 24 November 1646 (Venn). The references to Roger Bellwood in E. W. Crossley (ed.), op. cit. (item 41), p. 23, and in J. Charlesworth and A. V. Hudson (eds.), op. cit. (item 11), p. 64, are to the will of Josius Belwood. Another candidate, less likely in view of the dates, is John Belwood, vicar choral of York Minster 1620–49 (information from Bernard Barr).

APPENDIX 4

The Will of Anthony Foster
(BHI, Exchequer Probate Records, York City Deanery, July 1610)

In the name of god Amen the xjth daie of May in the yeare of o^r lord god one thousand six hundreth and tenne I Anthonie Foster of the Cittie of Yorke booke binder & beinge sicke in bodie yet of perfecte minde and memorie Thanckes be given to god I do ordaine and make this my last will and testament in manner and forme followinge. First I give and commend my soule into the mercifull hands of Almightie god my maker and redeemer trustinge thorough the mercies of Jesus Christe my onely sauior to have free remission of all my sinnes and to be fellow and heyre in his euer lastinge Kingdome and my bodie to bee buried in the north quire of St John [i.e., Michael le] Belfrie. Item I geve and bequeath vnto Anthonie Marsh sonne of Thomas Marsh twentie pounds of lawefull money of England. And my desire is that John Brice have the education of him. Item I geve to Margaret Marche xx.^{li} of lawefull money of England, and I will that Margaret my wyfe shall have the educacon of her. Item I geve to Willm Foster of london my brother foureteene poundes. Item I geve to Ellen the wife of Willm Crooth fortie shillings. Item whereas my brother Richard Foster doth owe me tenne pound due vnto mee at daies now past I geve the said some of tenne poundes vnto Ann, Isobell, and Brigett Foster daughters of my same brother Richard equallie to be deuided amongst them viz to each of them the some of iii^{li} vi^s viii^d. Item whereas Roger Jackman of yorke Stationer oweth vnto mee the some of eleuene poundes due vnto mee at daies now past I geve the same some of eleuen poundes to Anthonje Jackman his sonne and Margaret Jackman his daughter viz the somme of eight poundes to the said Anthonie and three poundes to the saide Margaret Item I geve vnto Agnes Marsh late wife of Thomas Marsh fortie shillings Item I geue to Robert Moore my servant xx^s Item I geue to Willm Foster my brothers sonne x^s Item I geue vnto Marie and John Brice eyther of them x^s. Item I geue to the children wth Alice Brice and Jane Jackman are now wth eyther of them fortie shillings a peece. If they bee borne aliue. Item I geue vnto Robert Holdsworth my best gowne. Item I geue vnto Alice Brice a golde ringe w a loade stone in it. Item I geue vnto Jane Jackman x^s. Item I geue vnto my brother John Foster the elder at London xx^s. Item I geue to Margaret his wyfe x^s Item I geue vnto Beatrice Clarke my seruant x^s Item I geue vnto John Foster now in the house wthine fortie poundes of lawfull English money Item I geue vnto my cosin Willm Foster now at Caimbrige x^s. The rest of all my goods and Chattells not formerlie giuen nor bequeathed my debts and legacies paied and my funerall discharged I giue vnto Margaret my wyfe whome I make my sole executrix of this my last will and testament. Item I will that my wyfe immediatlie after my decease shall suffer and permit my cosin John Foster now in howse wthin to have the vse and occupation of my shopp and all the wares bookes and other implements and working instruments in the same at the discretion of my wyfe during her life he dooinge and payinge for the same as he and she can agree, and I will that she deale better wth him therein then wth and other and that he have the same at an easie rate and better cheape then and other man so that he bee helpinge and assistinge to her; and I do further nominate and appointe Robt: Claphamson John Brice, and Roger Jackman of the Cittie of yorke supervisors of this my last will and testament as my trust is in them to see my will performed and I giue to each of them for their paines xx^s apeece and I do hereby annhillate revoke and make void all former wills by mee heretofore made. In wytness whereof I haue herevnto sett my hand and seale the day and yeare above written.

Witnesses hereof

Stephen Clarke	inv¹	13° Julii ibid probat Margarita
publique notarie		[illegible]¹
Robert Claphamson	inv¹	
Tho: Squire		

---

¹ The two words 'inv' alongside the names of the witnesses and three words which cannot be read beneath the date in the right-hand column are in another hand. If 'inv' against the names of Clarke and Claphamson is right, it may mean that they drew up the inventory, which has unfortunately been lost.

APPENDIX 5

The Will of Margaret Foster
(BHI, Probate Registers, vol. 32, fos. 392ᵇ–93ᵃ, March 1613)

In the name of God Amen the Nine and twentieth daie of March Anno domini 1613 I
Margarett Foster of the Cittie of Yorke Widow sicke in bodie yet of good & present
remembrance thankes be unto God, doe make this my last Will & Testament in
manner and forme followinge First I giue my soule into the handes of Allmightie god
my Creator & Redeemer trustinge assuredly by the merritts and death of Jesus Christ
my onely Saviour that all my sinnes are forgiven and that I shall reigne wᵗʰ him in his
everlastinge Kingdome and my bodie to be buried in Belfrey Church as neare my late
husband as conueniently maie be Item I giue vnto My Cosen John Foster Twentie
poundes wᶜʰ he oweth me as borrowed money wᶜʰ I lent him and should haue beene
repaid me long since Item I giue to the said John Foster the lease of my dwellinge
house in the Minster yarde wᵗʰ all shoppes and other houses and the Yard now
impayled belonginge vnto it and my right therein duringe his naturall liffe if the yeares
therein graunted doe soe longe Continue And if it please god to call him out of this
miserable Worlde before the Expiration of yᵉ said yeares in the said lease conteyned
then I giue the same lease for the yeares that shalle so endure after the liffe of the said
John Foster to Anthonie Jackman sonne of Roger Jackman of the Cittie of Yorke
Stacioner Item my will is that the said John Foster shall not surrender the said lease to
defraude this bequest to the said Anthonie Jackman and if he doe or goe aboute the
same then I will and my minde is that the same bequest of the lease aforenamed by me
to him giuen shalbe vtterlie voide and of none effect And then I giue the same lease
and all my right therein to Anthonie Jackman duringe the yeares therein to expire
Item I giue vnto my Godsonne Frauncis Brice the sonne of John Brice Ten poundes
Item I giue vnto Margarett Jackman daughter of Roger Jackman my Cosen seauen
pounds Item I giue to Ursuley and Matthew Jackman children of the said Roger
Jackman to either of them the Somme of Foure pounds Item whereas my late
husband did in his will giue to Anthonie Marsh and Margarett Marsh children of
Thomas Marsh deceased the Somme of Fortie poundes betwixt them either of them
xx.ˡⁱ I doe by this my Will give and bequeath to the said Anthonie Marsh and Margarett
Marsh the somme of Fortie poundes equally to be deuided betwixt them wᶜʰ in the
whole will extend to the somme of Foure score poundes wᶜʰ somme I haue lent to John
Brice vpon his bond of Eight score pounds to paie me Fower score pounds wⁱᵗʰin
six/teen/ daies after it shalbe demaunded And I doe giue ye said bond to the said
Anthonie and Margarett in lew of theire legacie of Fortie poundes giuen vnto them by
the will of my late husband Item I giue the Somme of Eight pounds to the poore to be
distributed at the direction of Robert Claphamson John Brice and Roger Jackman
And I will out of ye same shalbe giuen to ye poore prisoners in the Castle Fortie

[131] 107

shillinges And fortie shillinges to the Kidcoate Item I giue to Margarett Foster daughter of John Foster Stacioner Ten pounds Item I giue to William Wilkinson the somme of five poundes Item I giue to Ellen, Bridgett Issabell and Anne Foster children of Richard Foster of Staineforth the somme of Ten pounds owinge to me by theire Mother Item I giue to Thomas Foster my husbands eldest brother sonne Fortie shillinges & his brother William Foster xxx.ˢ Item my minde and will is that the wainescott glasse and dores and such as be affixed shall goe with the house and not be defaced alienated, or removed duringe the yeares of the lease Item I giue to Alice Brice one feather bed the best in the house, and the next feather bed I giue to Jane Jackman and the next Feather bed I giue to Joane Foster wiffe of John Foster And Another Feather bed to Margaret Marsh Item I giue to John Elizabeth and Mary Houldsworth the Children of Robert Houldsworth Fortie shillinges a peece Item I giue vnto the said Joane Foster wiffe of the said John Foster the Somme of Fiue pounds The rest of all my goods and Chattelles vnbequeathed I giue to Anthonie Marsh And Anthonie Jackman equallie betwixt them And I make them Executors of this my Will And I appointe Robert Claphamson my kinde friend Supervisor of this my Will and I desire him to see that my Executors doe performe this my Will and If anie legatorie or Executor be willfull and will not stand to and rest contented wᵗʰ this my Will att the discrecion of my said Superuisor I will yt the legacie or legacies to them giuen shalbe voide And I giue the said Robert Claphamson xx.ˢ in gould and to his wiffe a little ringe wᵗʰ a pansey And I giue to Jane Jackman my ringe wᵗʰ the Loadstone in it Item I giue to Peter Wilkinson and his wiffe an Angell of gould to either of them In Witnes whereof I haue heare vnto sette my hand & seale the day & Yeare aboue Written Witnesses thereof John Peirs & Robert Claphamson the thirtenth day of Aprill 1613 Item I giue vnto Alice Brice the somme of Ten poundes Item I giue to Jane Jackman a Coveringe of Arras worke and halfe a dosen of siluer spoones of the better sorte Item to my Cosen John Brice thother halfe dosen of spoones Item I giue to my Cosen John Foster Another halfe dosen of siluer spoones of the worst sorte Item I giue to George Dent wiffe xx.ˢ And I will that this Codicill be annexed to my Will witnesses hereof Robert Houldsworth and Robert Claphamson Et decimo octavo die mensis Maij Anno domini 1613 probatum tam Testamentum . . .